TERROR

IN THE

WOODS

True Stories

Steph Young

~~~

TABLE OF CONTENTS

Introduction

How can people just disappear in the Woods? How do others turn up dead in the woods, with no explanation?

The following true stories, set within the Woods or the most remote wilderness, encompass a baffling and puzzling combination of strange disappearances and inexplicable deaths, and the possible causes behind them.

One things that is certain, is that things are never quite what they seem....

Chapter 1: Strange coincidences among the Missing

A man owns a book-store in a small town surrounded by forest. He tells friends he's going on a short vacation with his dog. He never returns. Months later, a man opens an antiques store in the now former book store of the man who has vanished. The antiques dealer becomes fascinated by the story of the missing book-store owner and decides to write a book about it. Then he too disappears…

It was September 7th, 1987 when book-store owner Tom Young left his store in the quaint and picturesque former mining outpost of Silver Plume, in Clear Creek County, Colorado, population less than two hundred and often referred to as a 'ghost town.'

For those who knew the book-store owner, they all said that he was a pleasant and likeable man, whose constant companion was his dog, Gus. They'd often be seen walking around the small outpost and going for walks in the surrounding hills.

He told his friends and acquaintances that he was going to take a short vacation, and he was reported to have last been seen walking with his dog not far from his book-store. Others say he told them he was taking a hike. Whichever is the case, he never returned to his book-store....

A few months later, and a man moved into the same building that the now-closed book-store had been located in. His name was Keith Reinhard, and he opened an Antiques store. He'd actually been a professional writer before this move, writing a sports column for the Chicago Herald.

As soon as he heard of the strange disappearance of the former book-store owner and his dog, his curiosity was completely aroused. He decided he was going to write a fiction book, based upon the man's disappearance, and he began researching the case.

Only weeks later he was to find that the case of the missing man had a remarkable and very tragic ending. In July 1988, ten months after the book store owner had vanished, hunters came across the skeletal remains of a person, who appeared to be propped up against a tree in the middle of the mountains. A dog's remains lay close by, as did a handgun and a backpack.

The skull of the human remains was later determined to have a gunshot wound. It was also later determined that this was the missing book-store owner and his dog, and he was discovered to have purchased a gun only days before he disappeared. The dog too had been shot. For the Sheriff's department, it was a clear-cut case of suicide.

As for the locals however, who knew him so well, very few could even entertain the idea that this ordinarily happy and cheerful man had not only shot himself but his beloved dog too. They just couldn't believe he would do it.

The Sheriff's office did not see the need to run ballistic tests on the gun that was found. This left the question however; had he fired the shots? Or, had someone else perhaps? Given the recent purchase of the gun, the sheriffs were certain it had to have been a suicide. Perhaps he had merely bought the gun for his own protection however? It could have been grabbed from him and used against him by an assailant perhaps?

Had he been financially suffering from slow sales in a book-store with little passing trade, given its remote location? Did he have serious financial worries? His friends said he had certainly never intimated this to them if he did.

For Keith Reinhard, the former writer, this story had just got a lot juicier and he wanted to find out all he could about how and why the main character in the book he was writing had now been found dead in the forested mountains.

He wanted to go to the spot in which the man's body had been found, and he was determined to get there, and although the sports writer had no previous experience of hiking in the wilderness, this was not going to deter him. He told his family and friends of his intention and on the day he set out, they strongly advised him against it.

Not only was it not an easy hike, but he was leaving at gone 4 p.m. Given the distance he had to travel to get there and back, it would entail a round-trip of several hours, and could take up to 3 hours just to get to the spot.

This would certainly mean that his return trip would end up with him having to hike back in the dark. Despite this, and despite him taking no warm clothing for the evening and no backpack of supplies, he still set off, alone.

He didn't return. By the next day, helicopters were called in to search for him. A search party comprising of more than one hundred people and a number of tracker dogs, began to comb the forests and mountain in search of him.

Supervisor of the rescue team, Charley Shimanski later said that his search group had found every person who had ever gone missing in that area in the last three decades. As for this missing man however, he said; "He didn't leave many clues...He didn't have many with him to leave behind."

 He had no personal items that could have led a trail to him; no equipment or supplies, and, "This was about as difficult a search terrain as we cover," he said. "It is not an area for easy hiking. It's 3,000 vertical feet and a 60-degree slope." He was wearing tennis shoes when he set out.

Despite the search for the writer lasting over a week, they still could not find him, and a helicopter involved in the search also tragically crashed, killing the pilot. They could find no trace of him whatsoever, and to this day he is still missing. He was 57 then, he would be 87 now. More than 100 people searched for over 10,000 hours for him. They found no clues.

As to what happened to him, there are different versions of speculation. He planned to disappear and never did go on the hike; but that would have meant leaving his family behind, and he has never been in contact with them. He also, like the book-store owner, didn't appear to have any problems in his life.

Another version is that he had stumbled across something in his research about the missing book-store owner, that was dangerous for him to know and that he had been killed to silence him. Had the book store owner been murdered in the mountain and this writer killed because he was getting too close to uncovering his killer?

Or, was it a case of a terrible synchronicity and just coincidence that two men happened to die in precisely the same place, a year apart, while one was trying to discover what had happened to the first victim? A woefully unprepared man setting out on a hike to discover the fate of a man who had killed himself and his dog on the mountain? But if so, where was his body?

More than 100 people logged over 10,000 hours searching and never found a clue to what happened.

"Sometimes the answer is; there is no answer...." Reinhard's widow, Carolyn O'Donnell, told the Daily Herald.

~

In this next story, separated by several years, two brothers within the same family both vanished and have never been found. The first brother was 15-year-old Michael, youngest of three siblings in the Palmer family. He vanished in 1999, on June 4th, in Wasilla, in the Matanusak-Susitna Valley in Alaska.

He'd gone to a party with his school friends, and when they left to return home, somehow he simply vanished. He was riding a borrowed bicycle and they all set off together to ride home, approximately 9 miles from the party.

At some point on the journey home, his friends noticed that he was no longer cycling with them, and they pulled up at a late-night grocery store to wait for him to catch up with them. It was around 4 a.m. When he never arrived, they decided to continue their journey home without him.

The accounts from the boys differ over the years that have passed and according to the state troopers at the time the boy somehow got separated and they later said they assumed he had taken a different route to go home.

The police said that a bicycle later fished out of the Little Susitna River was his bicycle, although his brother said it was not the bike he had been riding. His brother also said that he heard there was a fight at the party.

After he was reported missing the following afternoon, divers thoroughly searched the river, about 50 searchers scoured the nearby woods, and the troopers questioned all the teenagers who had been at the party. The bicycle was found in the river which ran parallel to the road he had been cycling on. There was no sign of his body.

According to the report by the Charley Project Missing Person's website, his sneakers were discovered by a boy who had attended the same party. They were found on a private plane runway adjoined to a home, approximately 190 metres from the river. They were muddy and wet.

Rumours circulated that the missing boy had been involved in an altercation at the party, or that he was attacked and beaten while on his way home, by unidentified assailants. One local boy said he had watched him being thrown off the bridge having been shot, but later admitted he had invented the story.

Most local people theorized that the boy most likely fell into the river and drowned; however, the tracker dogs brought in quickly after his disappearance were unable to pick up his scent at the rivers-edge. The river was not frozen at that time of year and the water was still and clear.

No further evidence was ever found. No body, no other personal items belonging to the boy and no evidence of a crime having been carried out. His family were adamant there was simply no way he would have just upped and left in the middle of the night. He was a happy, normal boy, with friends, and no problems at school.

The family then began receiving phone calls, with the caller telling them that their son was dead. The police believed these were cruel hoax calls. The troopers found nothing to go on, and that was where his story ended, although they were at least confident that from the searches they'd carried out, he had not drowned in the river.

His friends took polygraphs tests, and passed. Their testimonies, while being polygraphed, supported what they had told the police when he was reported missing – that he had set out from the party to ride home with them. Somehow, eerily, without these boys even hearing anything, he disappeared among them, and has never been found.

His sneakers were found on a private plane runway adjoined to a home, approximately 190 metres from the river. Why were his sneakers off? Did the police check for any aircraft in the vicinity? Was he snatched and flown somewhere?

Fast-forward to 11 years later and his two remaining siblings, now adults, planned to go with a group of their friends and relations on a snowmobile trip into the Talkeetna Mountains. It was April time, and they drove to the cabin approximately one hour away from their home, amid the snowy craggy slopes of the Mountain.

After arriving at the cabin, the group decided to go for a ride on their snowmobiles. It was now already dark. Just before they set out however, the eldest of the brothers had to pull out, after the handlebars of his snowmobile broke and he had no choice but stay behind. The elder brother, Chuck, went ahead with the group and in an eerie turn of events, he too would never return home.

In the dark, they set out on their machines, and at some point during their ride, he became separated from the rest of the group, and was never seen again. He simply didn't return to the cabin.

The *Alaska Daily News* reported that Chuck Palmer was riding a new machine he'd only recently purchased, and that it was believed the other men in the group had gone at a faster pace than he, and he had been left behind at some point. His older brother blamed himself, telling the newspaper that he would ordinarily be in the back of the group, making sure everyone kept up and stayed together. He said the other men were more experienced with their machines and his brother hadn't been able to keep up the pace with them.

The men later said that the last time they saw him, he was riding off in the wrong direction, away from them. The group said that after seeing him riding off in the opposite direction they had tried to call him but he didn't hear them, the roar of his snowmobile presumably drowning out their voices. His brother sat up all night, expecting him to return at any moment but he never did.

Nearly 50 search and rescue trackers arrived to search for the missing man the next morning. His snowmobile was found the following day, but there was no sign of him, and even more strange, there were no sign of any footprints in the area. The area in which his vehicle was found abandoned was off the main trail and waist-deep in snow.

There were no footprints around the vehicle. This oddity led the fire chief of a near-by town, who was there with the rest of the official searchers, to comment that it was as though the missing man had been "shanghaied by a passing UFO," because he could find no other logical explanation for the fact that there were no footprints there.

The search continued for weeks. No-one could believe he simply wouldn't be found. He had to have been close to his snowmobile - the snow was too deep for him to have got that far away.

When June came and the warmer weather resulted in a thaw on the mountain, planes flew overhead, expecting to spot the man's remains, but when still no body could be found, the authorities came to the only conclusion they could; that natural predators had eliminated all trace of the man, that his body had to have been consumed by natural predators.

While this is indeed the most logical conclusion, the mystery remains about the lack of footsteps. Had the snow merely covered his footfall around his abandoned vehicle, so greatly that even the most experienced of trackers couldn't detect them? And yet they could not pick up his trail, at all.

However, supervisor of the searchers, Sergeant Troy Shuey, did point out; "We've had 28 inches of snow since the search started." Had he succumbed to hypothermia and died? It is very likely the most plausible explanation, given that the snow was over waist-deep and falling.

Yet, there's also the fact that he simply could not have got too far away from his abandoned vehicle, because walking in snow that deep would not be an easy thing to do at all. No person could walk for miles in waist-high snow His body should have been found in a very small radius then, but it wasn't....

Chapter 2: Two boys, Two missing shoes.

On October 23, 1981, 17-year-old Kurt Sova went to a party a few blocks from his family home with friend Samuel Carroll in the small rural town of Newburgh Heights, Ohio. The party was being held at the rented apartment of brother and sister, Clayton and Debbie Sams. It was a Halloween party. Kurt had been drinking that night and perhaps too much, because it was said he began to become unsteady and bump into things, and so his friend Samuel took him outside for some air.

Once outside, his friend Samuel said that Kurt vomited, and he left him hanging onto a fence while he went back inside to collect their jackets because it was chilly outside. When he came back outside, having been away he estimates for no more than 2 or 3 minutes, Kurt was gone.

Samuel did a 360, looked all around, searched the nearby streets and went over to the Furniture Warehouse a few hundred metres away to search the parking lot there. Unable to find him however, he assumed that his friend must have gone home, and so he returned to the party.

By the next morning, Kurt's mother and father were out looking for him, having realized he didn't come home the night before.

Two days after the party, the police began to look for him. His mother spoke to the girl who had held the party, and she told her that her son wasn't there. A pizza delivery boy however clearly remembered seeing Kurt there, when he delivered pizzas to the party. Kurt's jacket was also found inside the house.

His mother and father began to plaster missing person's posters all over the neighbourhood and up to fifty people searched the garages, dumpsters, alleys, and ravines looking for the missing teenager.

Two days later, a homeless man walked into a record shop in the small town. He'd been hanging around outside it for a couple of weeks. The homeless said that he had "access to bodies flown in" to the nearby Cleveland Hopkins International Airport. He bragged about stealing the shoes from the bodies.

This day, he walked up to the store manager Judy Oros, and pointed to Kurt's missing person's poster on display in the store window. He tells her; "They're going to find him and they're going to find him in two days and they're not going to know what happened to him."

The following day, the girl who hosted the party told Kurt's family that their missing son had been sleeping in a cot down in the basement of the house in which they rented their apartment. His father and brothers went to the basement of the house and kicked the door in. His father believed that it looked like someone had been sleeping there recently, but there was no sign of his missing son.

The next day, three kids cut through the woods behind the furniture store on their way home from school. They spot what looks like a discarded shop mannequin, half-in and half-out of the river. The body is posed in a crucifixion.

According to Cleveland newspaper The Plain Dealer, the body was "cruciform, arms outstretched, head to one side, one knee slightly bent and one foot atop the other." Patrolman Paul T. Grzesik said, "When we arrived there, his body was laid out like Christ on the cross. One shoe was found nearby. We never found the other (right) shoe."

It wasn't a mannequin at all; it was Kurt's body. He was dressed, but both of his shoes were missing. Eventually, the right shoe would be found positioned in a pile of rocks nearby.

The coroner later determined that he had a bruise on his cheek, bruises on his shins and minor abrasions. He had no knife wounds, no bullet wounds, no needle marks, and no internal injuries. His feet had no injuries to them, and they did not appear as though he had been walking without shoes on. The coroner was unable to find a cause of death.

The next day, the homeless man goes back into the record store. He has a bunch of flowers. He wants to give them to the store manager, but she has not arrived at work yet, so he hands them to the assistant to give to her. With the flowers is a card. It reads: "Roses are red, the sky is blue, they found him dead and they'll find you."

When the store manager arrives, she calls the police. They question the homeless man but they find no cause for arresting him. After this, he is never seen again.

Three days after Kurt disappeared, and prior to his body being found in the ravine, a friend of his, David Trunsnik, was en-route to a job interview. He was driving when he spotted Kurt, accompanied by a man he did not know. He slowed down his car to pull over and offer Kurt a ride and then watched as a van he also did not recognise, pulled up and he heard Kurt shout out "Franco," then watched as Kurt got into the van with the man who was accompanying him.

Mrs Angelina Reddicks, a local resident, came forward many months later to say that she saw, from her bedroom window, 2 males dragging a teenage boy like he was unconscious, toward the ravine where Kurt's body was found. She said her husband advised her not to speak out, not to get involved, out of fear of repercussions.

The police investigation of the case was labelled a joke by many subsequent law enforcement bodies. One officer on the force at the time was later jailed for using excessive force against people he questioned, although this was not related to the boy's death. Crime scene photos of Kurt's body, which had been left in what clearly looked like a deliberately posed crucifixion, were not taken, or if they were, they do not exist now. Proper examination of the crime scene was also alleged to have been woefully inadequate.

Theories about what happened to Kurt range from the most obvious; too much alcohol, or, that he took or was given drugs which caused him to become comatose and he was placed in the basement to cool off and recover, or rather, that he overdosed, and the teens at the party panicked and did not know what to do with his body.

That they placed him in the basement of the house and he was then moved from the basement to the ravine a few days later. Certainly, he was not in the ravine from the night he died, because his father had been over that ravine and the surrounding locality with a fine-tooth comb, including the night before his son's body was found there. He was most certainly placed there, but not on the night he disappeared.

Was the crucifixion merely a very deliberate distraction, to make it appear that this was a religious nut lone killer? And yet, how did Kurt die if the medical examiner could find no cause? His body was tested for LSD and cocaine. Maybe it was a different kind of drug, one far less regularly tested for? His autopsy did determine that he had died no more than 1 to 1 ½ days prior to being found.

His father, sadly now deceased, felt it may have been at the hands of a teenage local gang of delinquents who called themselves "brick city outlawz." The teenage boy could very easily have become involved in a scuffle that turned into a fight that got out of hand and killed him. He had abrasions to his shins. The coroner however didn't find sufficient injury to his body that would have resulted in fatal wounds.

Some say it must have been a serial killer, who took the one missing shoe as a trophy. Why was the other one found wedged in a pile of rocks? The location at which they left his body was a regularly travelled route for local kids. It was inevitable that he would have been found very quickly when placed there. Did the killer/s not care? Or, again, was there a deliberate reason for this; that they wanted him to be found this way?

If the witness Mrs Reddicks had seen him being dragged by two men, were his shoes on at the time, did they come off while being dragged? His feet showed no signs of walking barefoot nor of any abrasions or injury.

Who was the homeless man? And how did he know exactly when the missing boy would be found? and even more curiously, how did he know they would not know how he died? It appears he threatened or gave a not-so-subtle warning to the female record store owner that she would be next, and yet, no harm came to her. Had the homeless man somehow overheard what had happened to the boy being discussed by the killers?

But what did this have to do with his bragging about stealing shoes off presumably dead bodies being flown into the airport? Why would dead bodies be flown regularly into the airport? How did they die and where were the bodies coming from, if true?

As well as this strange story about the regional airport, we also have the proximity of the infamous Wright-Patterson Air-force base, located approximately 3 hours away. Infamous because of all the rumours about the base, since the late 1940's. Tales of crashed UFO's and alien bodies secretly transported from Roswell to the base.

What allegedly happened in the desert in New Mexico and was then apparently transported straight to the Air-Force base and placed inside a hanger that was denied access event to Senators? There are the accounts of supposed former employees of the base, suggestions that a maze of subterranean tunnels and vaults lie beneath the ground, and in these vaults lies alien technology and worse.

Hangar 18 in particular is said to be sealed to all but a very few who can get clearance to go inside. Long have been the claims that secret deals with alien races have resulted in agreements by our Governments to exchange human beings in return for these advances in technology; Humans offered as gifts for the advancement of technology.

Investigative journalist, Press Grey, has been looking into this case and according to their Project Astral, projectastral.net, one year prior to Kurt's disappearance and discovery, on October 28th, 1980, an hour from where he was found, at Pepper Lake, a brother and sister were out walking when they later reported that they were approached by a black disc-shaped metallic object in the sky, with bright lights in the middle of it.

It was silent as it flew toward them, and roughly around the month that Kurt disappeared, (no exact date given) in Painesville, Ohio, less than 30 minutes from where Kurt disappeared, a man observed a triangular object flying over Lake Erie, which he estimated to be an astonishingly 2 stories high, and again, this huge object was silent.

From other UFO records, on ufoinfo.com, is a report of another incident also in October 1981, in which a man was out at around 11 pm when he witnessed a triangle shaped object, with lights on the sides of the craft and that "seemed big enough to be 2 stories high, about, 70 ft. long at a guess and slightly smaller in the back. I have seen it more than once."

He continues, "I've never told a soul what I'm about to say here. I am opening this up for anyone to comment. All I ask is be kind as this is not easy for me. I am also going to try to give as much detail as possible. I have thought long and hard lately about how to write this down so I'll start at the beginning and end at the end. A little about me, I live near Cleveland Ohio, but in a suburb. This happened about 25 to 28 years ago."

"I remember it like it was yesterday, at least parts of it. There are no lights on my street. My mom had remarried, I had my bedroom to myself. I never liked the window shades open. I have double shades on now (I'm back at the house). That night was hot, so I had the window opened. Something woke me up, I was a sound sleeper; but no more. I went to the window even though I had no idea what woke me. To my left, east of the

Lake there was a ship. That's what I'm going to call it. It was a UFO to me, since I have no idea what it was.

We had a large back yard, and no houses built behind, just a lot of woods. It was moving very slowly. I was thinking a helicopter, but it didn't have that shape, nor was there any sound. It looked like it had a spotlight, going back and forth across the ground. That's about the time I saw the second ship, this time coming over the trees and much closer. It also had a light searching the ground in the same fashion. Then, all of a sudden, the light flew right up in my face. I'm not sure if my legs went out or I ducked or both! I woke in my bed, the next morning.

Shortly after that, "......" came to live with us, with twin beds now in my room. Here started five weeks of weird things. I woke up one night just like before - there was the same ship. Light in the window, and then the next thing I know "....." is waking me up early in the morning. I was outside on a lawn-chair sleeping!

Now how on earth did the chair get off the pool? - we have an above ground pool, it's locked and the key is inside the back door. We keep it locked. When I woke, I was in my jammies and the key was where it was supposed to be. This episode repeated itself several times that summer. P.S. I've had a terrible time with the computer this morning it kept shutting off when I was trying to start up and turn off a few times when I was writing this...'

In October 1981, in Rock Creek, Ashtabula County, Ohio, one hour from where Kurt disappeared, Press Grey of Project Astral found an account of three young men in a wooded area who suddenly noticed a huge black form step out from the tree-line onto the abandoned railroad tracks. They estimated it was approximately 20 feet away. The creature, whatever it was, suddenly began running toward them at a high rate of speed. Terrified, they fled in panic. The next day, odd shaped footprints were found where the creature had been.

Whether this is the same account or another one, also in October 1981 in the same area, three men including former army sergeant Todd M. Neiss were in a wooded area one evening when they began to hear strange sounds and brush around them breaking. A creature then suddenly stuck its head out the tree-line running alongside the abandoned railroad tracks. In a panic, one of the young men shot at the creature.

The creature fell down among the bushes, presumably having been shot, but got back up again, and ran into the woods, screaming as it did so. The young men described the creature as being very odd in appearance. They said it appeared to have one eye way off to the side of its face.

These were not the only accounts of unidentified creatures in this area. Prior to this, approximately 75 minutes away, in February 1981, at 2 a.m., a married woman claimed she was abducted by 'humanoids' and a UFO was reported, flying over the area of a flooded gravel pit. In April, at 3. 54 a.m. a dog owner also reported their animal became extremely agitated and there was the appearance of a very bright light which hovered over the woods, moving up and down.

According to Project Astral, in 2015 alone, Ohio had 2,907 confirmed UFO sightings, often close to Wright-Patterson. They ask, could UFO/Paranormal activity have been a cause for the lengthy disappearance and the placement of Kurt's body within the same area he went missing? Or, is there a much more mundane reason for his body to have been missing?

 "We searched the ravines, searched the schoolyards. I even went so far as to search dumpsters looking for him," his mother said.

Some reports from teenage friends implied that Kurt may have been drinking an alcoholic beverage called 'Everclear' which was an incredibly strong drink, and in fact led to the death of at least one person before it was banned for sale; however, the Coroner stated; "He didn't have enough alcohol to end his life."

If he had been very drunk, as his friend Samuel certainly believed he was that night, perhaps he wandered off in a stupor, could have been hit by a car, and in shock, had wandered off and fallen into a ravine, and died of hypothermia. This probably could not have been the case, however, as he had no injuries other than slight bruising, and the coroner would have been able to rule on hypothermia if it had been present in his body. Also, as his father pointed out, the area he was found in had been searched multiple times. "We were in teams. We must have had 40 people looking for him - day and night," his mother, Dorothy Sova recalled. His father said he had searched the ravine in which Kurt was found, only hours before his body was found, and the ravine had been empty.

Had he been sleeping/dead in the cot in the basement of the house in which the party had been held, all the time? Then taken to the ravine? Why was his body found deliberately placed in a crucifix shape?

Bill Sammon, reporter for the Plain Dealer newspaper, wrote that 'his body was cruciform, arms outstretched, head to one side, one knee slightly bent.'

"When we arrived there, his body was laid out like Christ on the cross," said Paul T. Grzesik, who was a part-time patrolman at the time. "One shoe was found nearby. We never found the other (right) shoe."

In January 1982, three months after Kurt's body was found, schoolboy Eugene Kvet was found dead in a ravine 2.5 miles from the ravine in which Kurt's body had been found. His right shoe was also missing. He had been missing for roughly the same amount of time as Kurt.

His cause of death was 'presumed' as 'falling,' into the ravine, although of course, he could have been pushed, or thrown. Eugene knew Kurt. Eugene, like Kurt is thought to have had only minor abrasions.

Why were two boys found dead in ravines close-by, with one missing shoe, and their deaths unable to be logically explained?

Chapter 3: The Missing & the "Starlight Tours."

20-year-old Christina Calayca, from Toronto, Canada, had gone camping to Rainbow Falls Provincial Park, near Thunder Bay in Ontario when she vanished without trace on August 6th, 2007. She had gone with three friends from her church group. She had left her friends to go for a jog, but never returned to camp.

On August 13th, approximately eighty police and volunteers searched the north shore of Lake Superior. Divers searched the lakes but turned up nothing. The following day, side-scan sonar was brought in to survey the water. Police Chief superintendent told reporters: "Side-scan sonar is towed along the bottom by our underwater search and recovery teams and give us an image of anything that is on the bottom." Nothing was found.

Aircraft, marine units and 3 canine teams had also been combing the rough terrain and densely wooded area, in clear weather. A 17-day search was carried out after she vanished. Then, another week-long search, bringing in a high-angle team who scaled the cliff edges for any sign of the body of the missing young woman.

A year after she vanished, her mother, Elizabeth Rutledge, mounted an independent ten-day search, costing her $40,000. It included cadaver dogs. Interviewed by The Star Newspaper, she noticed a strange man walking his cat on a leash at the beach. Did he snatch her daughter, she wondered?

At the campground, rakes and shovels hang on wooden posts for campers to use. Could someone have buried Christina? Nicole Baute for the Toronto Star wondered. There were drag racers in the park that weekend. Were any of them involved? - her mother could only speculate and try to come up with ideas, all of which would not bring her daughter back to her alive.

Her daughter had reportedly last been seen by her friend, Eddy Migue, on the 6th of August, after their first night at the camp. She had left him to go for her run. They were both members of a Church group in Toronto, and it was later said that none of them knew much about the outdoors.

The park was busy that weekend, with the vast majority of its camping sites booked up. Many of the campers were from local towns but some were from farther afield who had come for the Dragfest, which attracts up to 10,000 spectators and participants. Other campers would have been stopping off temporarily while traveling along the Trans-Canada Highway, otherwise known to some as the Highway of Tears, which runs right through the park. The highway was less than a kilometre from the park gates just off the Trans-Canada, with short hiking trails and a couple of beaches on the Lake.

The missing woman's first cousin, Faith Castulo, and two friends from a Church Youth Group, Edward, and Joe went with her to the forest. Christina was a leader of the Youth Group and spent much of her time helping out and volunteering with the ministry.

The morning after they had arrived, Christina and Eddy were awake before their friends, and feeling refreshed and excited to be there they were up just after dawn. While their companions slept in, they decided to go for a jog.

Eddy was more of a runner than Christine, and its believed that she had a sore foot at the time from a previous minor injury. As they set out on the run, Eddy wanted to run along the Highway but Christine, perhaps thinking that would be too much for her, decided to run inside the park along one of the short trails.

With a few campers emerging from their tents by now to go for showers, Eddie and Christine separated and without fixing a time to meet back up, they set off on their respective jogs. He later said that he saw her walking away as he set off on his run, and that she was headed to the trail that would lead to the waterfall. Eddie was gone for perhaps an hour, during which time he at some point stopped to carve their initials on a rock and ran on again. He estimates he was away from the camp for about an hour.

When he returned to their camping spot, his friends were still sound asleep, and he sat in a chair and fell off to sleep himself. Approximately a couple of hours later, his two friends finally woke up. At this point, Christine had been gone for about 3 hours. Her cousin and friend asked Eddie where she was, and they reasoned that she must be taking her time along the trail, enjoying being out in the wilderness. Her friend, J.B. looked along the beach on his way back from the shower, but didn't spot her there.

When they all were back at the tent, they decided to take the car along the road toward the waterfall to see if she was there, so two of them got in the car, while one of them searched a larger hiking trail. By 2 p.m. their searches for her had proved fruitless, and now at the park gate, about to drive around some more to search for her, they asked the parks attendant for a map of the trails. He asked if he could help them and they said they had lost their friend.

They said they were headed to the end of a 12km trail to look for her there, but the parks attendant said he doubted she would have walked that far. He became concerned when he heard how long she had been gone and he said they should call the police. He then made the call for them.

While awaiting the arrival of the provincial police, the park service began a search of the trails and beach. It was not long before the police came. Within a couple of hours, a full-scale search was underway, headed by the Emergency Response team. Over the next 24 hours, this was to include 4 helicopters, 4 dog units, and 100 searchers including trained search volunteers, sonar mapping for underwater search and infra-red cameras to detect on land.

Searchers shouted her name constantly, hoping to hear her reply. The dogs began their search where she had separated from Eddie that morning but according to Kate Barker's report for ExploreCanada; 'Canine units are most effective when deployed on a calm, warm day when the scent isn't carried away on the wind or doesn't evaporate in the cold. The conditions were perfect. But the dogs ideally need to be tracking within the first 12 hours. The dogs were working on a 24-hour deficit by the time they arrived, and no scents were detected.'

The searchers covered the Waterfall area, the beaches and all of the trails. Over the days that followed, they would cover over 50 kilometres. Overhead searches each day looked for any signs she might have left if she had got into trouble, been injured or got stuck somewhere, but they saw no signs. Her family had arrived soon after the alarm was raised. They began to believe something sinister must have happened to her.

They couldn't see her wandering off deep into the woods. Kate Barker's report reveals she was afraid of spiders, and only a few weeks before this, she had been with some friends when they'd got lost on a hiking trail – her family said that the experience shook her up so much she had begun praying to God to let them get out of there alive. They couldn't imagine she would have now gone so far off the beaten track, alone.

Had she been attacked by a bear, people wondered? The police flew in a Bear specialist. He said he would have spotted the signs if there had been a bear attack; drag marks, blood, broken branches.

Her family wondered, was she taken from the park shortly after she had gone for her run? Had someone accosted her, made a grab for her? Had she been limping perhaps, because of her foot problem, had someone slowed their car down and offered her a ride back to camp, on the pretext of being a good Samaritan? with Christine feeling the alternative was a long painful walk back, had she let her guard down momentarily and accepted the ride? It would have taken just moments to get back out on the Highway from the trail.

Her friends were interviewed several times but the police found nothing to suggest any involvement by them. The alternative could have been that she had planned to disappear, but no-one who knew her felt this to be at all realistic. She loved her Youth Group, she loved her job as a day-care assistant, she had plans for her future, and on top of that, there would have been far easier ways to disappear than to go off into the forest with no purse or any other items she would need.

She is still missing. The Highway which runs past the forest, runs for miles and this Trans-Canada Highway is other-wise known as The Highway of Tears. It spans the length of Canada, snakes past thick forests, logging towns and impoverished Indian reserves on its way to the Pacific Ocean, and it runs right through the park from which she vanished. To date, estimates are that more than 50 women have disappeared from this Highway.

This is how it became known as the Highway of Tears. The New York Times in 2016, reported on the continuing situation. 'Dozens of women vanish on the Highway of Tears; most cases are unsolved.' It lists several examples.

'Less than a year after her 15-year-old cousin vanished, Delphine Nikal, aged 16, was last seen hitching from her isolated northern town one morning in 1990.' She has never been found. 'Ramona Wilson, aged 16, left home one Saturday evening in 1994 to go to a dance a few kilometres away.' She is still missing. 'Tamara Chipman aged 22, was last seen hitching on the Highway in 2006.' Nicole Hoar, 25, was working as a tree planter in 2002 when she vanished from the Highway.

Community activists say the numbers of missing is up in the 50's. Signs can now be seen along the roadside, saying, "Don't Hitchhike" and even "Killer on the loose."

In May 2011 Madison Scott vanished near the highway. She'd been at a party in a camp and her tent and car were still there, but she had disappeared without trace, and is still missing. Her family told a reporter for *Vanderhoof Omineca Express*, "She had her head screwed on. We don't think she just wandered off drunk and fell into the lake. It is completely out of character."

Some women have been found dead, by the road side or in the depths of the forest. Some of the missing women were found to have been the victims of serial killer Bobby Fowler, possibly as many as nine women. Others may have been victims of the serial killer Robert Pickton. As to the many remaining women still missing, their fates are unknown. The police have no clues as to what might have happened to them.

Pickton was implicated in the murder of Dawn Teresa Crey, who was reported missing in December 2000. Pickton owned a pig farm, and was reported to have been a multi-millionaire. He apparently was alleged to have held wild parties on his farm, during which some particularly terrible things may have taken place.

Certainly, he has confessed to killing women on his farm, mainly prostitutes, and then feeding their bodies to his pigs. In 2007, he was convicted of killing six women, however, from DNA of human remains found on his farm, 33 other women are believed to have been killed by him there too.

Even more shocking and perhaps completely impossible to really believe, is the allegation from former fighter pilot Field McConnell, also known as 'Abel Danger,' an investigator and author and who runs a YouTube channel under this name, along with his cambridge educated partner David Hawkins. They believe they have discovered the most astonishing and horrifying details, which in their opinions, prove much more was going on at this farm than has been publicly released.

It's a most intricate and complex web of tales, but it somehow involves the filming of Snuff movies and a remote spread-betting ring involving politicans and the wealthy, who would bet on the timing of each woman's death while watching it happen live, remotely. The stuff of wild speculation and fevered imagination? – it certainly could be.

"Pay-per-view snuff-film betting following a Dark Web model for Piggy's Palace charity launched in 1996 at the Pickton Family pig farm in British Columbia," says Abel Danger. "Allegedly move furloughed prisoners through raves at the Pickton pig farm, and establish a vig based on the time they took to disappear a prostitute's body.... in a wood chipper." Abel's actual name is Field McConnell and he is "offering to serve as an expert witness in any action for wrongful deaths."

He has, he believes, much credible information about any number of quite possibly interconnected major events. Pure fantasy? – very likely, and indeed, it doesn't appear connected to missing women such as Christina.

So perhaps while their alleged information may seem one step too far in terms of reality, there have also been totally unrelated allegations of something called "Starlight tours," along the 'Highway of Tears.' In a forum, a woman relates the story told to her by her aunt, in which her aunt tells her that a few years ago, when she was younger, she ended up getting very drunk. One night at a local bar, a cop who happened to be near-by, noticed this and told her he'd be taking her to jail overnight to sober up. She complied with his instructions and got into the cop car.

Not long after getting into the car she passed out. When she woke up, an estimated 15 minutes later, she looked out the car window and noticed that they had gone past the jail. She quickly asked the policeman why he'd driven past the jail only for him to apparently let out a big sigh, which she interpreted to mean he was irritated or frustrated by her comment. He immediately turned the car around and proceeded to take her directly to the jail. Looking back on that night, the aunt said she always gets the chills thinking about it, and wondering, could it have anything to do with all the missing women along the Highway.

Of course, this is just one woman's story, who happened to be drunk at the time, so perhaps we could easily dismiss it, however, the reality of "Starlight Tours" cannot so easily be dismissed. The "Saskatoon freezing deaths" were a real occurrence back in the 2000's, of mainly indigenous men, who were allegedly picked up by police for drunkenness and driven in their police cars out into the wilderness and left there, often in the dead of winter. Some allegedly died as a result, including

Rodney Naistus, Neil Sontechild, and Lawrence Wegner. Stonechild's body was found frozen. Wegner's body was also found frozen to death near a dump. Naistus was found frozen to death five days before that.

Canada's National Magazine reported; "The body of an Indian man was found near the power plant, in bone-chilling temperatures. Five days later, another body, frozen solid was found. He was wearing just jeans and a T-shirt. What would he be doing so far out of town with no jacket and no shoes? And what would anybody be doing that far out of town, period, in the middle of winter?" He'd last been seen downtown.

For years, it had been rumours, a local urban myth; that was, until the bodies began to be found. One young man, "Lyle" told the newspaper, he was driven out of town. "They pulled over to this driveway into a field. The cops got out and opened the door. One shook me by my jacket, then told me, "You have 20 seconds," and I was like, "for what?" He answered, "To run. Run into that field." I got really scared, I didn't ask any more questions I just started running."

Two police officers, although not found guilty of causing death, were imprisoned on the grounds of false confinement, and while the police said these were isolated incidents, the Chief of Police also later admitted that there was a possibility these practices had been going on for some time, when a woman was found to have been driven out of the city to the wilderness and abandoned there as far back as 1976.

When Neil Stonechild was picked up he was drunk, as was his friend. When the police put Stonechild in the police car, they turned and asked his friend Jay if he knew Neil. Jay lied and said he didn't know him – he had a warrant out for his own arrest and he wanted to get out of there fast. The police accepted what he told them, but he said his friend Neil was screaming in the back of the police car, yelling to his friend that they were going to kill him.

That is what haunts Jay now. This was the last time he saw his friend. His friend's body was found frozen to death five days later. What surprised Jay the most at the time was that Neil too had a warrant for his own arrest – the police should have taken him to jail, and kept him in. Instead they took him for a long ride.

Chapter 4: The Missing & the found Feet.

While in the cases of Kurt Sova and Eugene Kvet, both were missing a shoe, other people it seems, are missing their feet. Also in Canada again, the Guardian newspaper asked in 2016, "After four years, why are more feet washing ashore in British Columbia? Since 2007, 12 human feet clad in running shoes have been found on the shores of British Columbia. At Botanical Beach, in British Columbia, multiple feet have been discovered. Human feet that have been washing up on its shores for the last nine years!'

It had been nearly four years since a foot sighting, and then on February 7th, a new foot washed up on-shore, discovered by a hiker along Vancouver Island's Botanical Beach. Five days later, another one appeared. After so many years, the arrival of human feet on the province's shores was old news, but when they started to be discovered in 2007, speculation about where they came from ran rampant.

A *Toronto Star* article suggested theories ranged from natural disasters, like the Tsunami, to the result of drug dealers, serial killers, or human traffickers to alien abductions. The Coroner at the time, Ms McLintock, said it was not the work of a serial killer, nor of "alien abductions" and that all the identified individuals committed suicide or died accidentally, most likely as a result of storms near the coast, and that the feet naturally separate from the body as a process of decomposition, and that it happens faster if in water than on dry land.

 "The forensic anthropologists can be really sure of that because they can tell looking at the ends of the bones whether they disarticulated naturally or whether there's any sign that any mechanical force has been applied to them, whether there's any trauma, whether there's any tool marks on them," she said. "And none of them have had anything like that. All the evidence pointed to this natural articulation process."

But why did the feet only start turning up in 2007? And, have there been other occurrences elsewhere, as suggested by a person called 'Papa Crocodile,' as we shall see in a minute. The coroner suggests this new phenomenon of feet is due to new design technology which enable a lighter form of foot-wear, allowing for ease of floating to the surface more readily.

We have the statement from the coroner that most of the feet have been identified, but we also have the strange phenomenon of many of the feet being right feet. Why would this be? The coroner said there is no evidence on these feet of them having been chopped or hacked or cut or snapped off with implements or machinery or weapons. And yet, we also have the quandary that many were right feet, which could simply be coincidence, but added to the fact that no other parts of the body were or are ever found?

The Washington Post said, in 2016; "Sixteen detached human feet have been found since 2007 in British Columbia, Canada, and Washington state. Most of these have been right feet. All of them were wearing running shoes or hiking boots, including two 'Nikes,' 'New Balances,' and 'Ozark Trail.'

The most recent one turned up that week, in February 2016. The Stevens family were taking a walk on Vancouver Island when the husband spotted something in the sand. It looked like a shoe. A closer inspection revealed "an actual foot bone in it."

Regional coroner, Matt Brown said the exact model of shoe had been released for sale after March 2013, indicating that the person it belonged to must have gone missing after 2013. After the first two feet, both right feet, were found in British Columbia within a six-day period, local people and the authorities expressed concern. Five more were found the next year.

Two of the feet were since identified as having belonged to people with mental illness, while three more were linked to individuals who "probably died of natural causes."

"Of the ones identified so far, there's no mystery," criminologist at British Columbia's Simon Fraser University Gail Anderson said in 2011. "These people were depressed, and were last seen heading toward the water."

Forensic consultant Mark Mendelson however, begs to differ. He told the Daily Beast in 2011; "Everybody who jumps off a bridge is wearing runners? Until you can show me something pathologically concrete that this is a natural separation of that foot from a body, then I'm saying you've got to think dirty."

Cpl. Garry Cox of the Oceanside Royal Canadian Mounted Police said at the time; "Two in such a short period of time is quite suspicious. Finding one is like a million to one odds," Cox said, "but to find two feet is crazy, come on…"

Well, is it all something and nothing, or, could there really be something very sinister and nefarious going on?

'Papa Crocodile' is a Priest of Palo Mayombe. (Palo Mayombe originated from the African Congo and is said to be one of the world's most powerful forms of dark magic and sorcerery.) He has written of the phenomenon of the missing feet and he believes it may tie-in to the many unsolved cases of missing people in wilderness areas.

He says that the explanation for the feet being "people fallen over-board" is for him, an unsatisfactory answer. "Fish eating all but the one foot?" he queries. -His point being, that if the rest of the body is not found and is presumed to have been eaten by sharks or fish, then wouldn't the right (usually) severed foot have been eaten too?

Of the feet discovered, the majority are the right foot, and feet belonging to men. He says that this is not the first time it has happened. 'Being from Southern California, I remember in the late 1980's human feet washing up along the coastline. These were quickly attributed to shark attacks and the issue never reported on again.'

'There has also supposedly been "hoax" feet found as well,' he says, which serve perhaps as a distraction from taking it seriously or as anything more than the given reason. 'Drop the mention of a hoax,' he writes, 'I decided I would take occult approaches. I will ask an M'pungo (a deity spirit from the Congo) or a spirit of the dead, to look into this situation and I would see through their eyes.'

'I would also perform a magical divination - I would go to the ultimate expression of true primordial oceanic prowess…Leviathan, and ask her to take me on a spiritual exploration of the ocean.'

The results of this he says are, 'I was shown a young boy being held down by French colonialists in a diamond mine and his foot being chopped off with an axe. - This was common practice in the 1800's. Instead of killing slaves attempting to escape, they cut off their foot so they could still work but not run. I was then shown a flotilla of a few yachts, in international waters. I was shown what was inside the barges. They seemed to be floating heroin production centres. Armed men standing watch over a large group of naked men and women with one of their feet removed and chained to a table'.

'These are kidnapped slaves, kept and worked until they die. I was then shown something that disturbed me even further. Their teeth had been removed, or knocked out. Their captors looked like steroid-fuelled monsters.. so biting them would seem useless. Next my attention was taken to an earlier time, where slaves would commit suicide by biting their own tongues off and bleeding to death. That seemed to indicate why the teeth were removed; they wanted you alive as long as possible.'

'I was then shown what was on the Yachts. Drugs, alcohol, sex slaves, dog fighting, all manner of entertainment. Even for the most depraved individual, being around that much abject human misery can wear on the vilest minds, and full immersion

into human vice and debauchery would be needed for cathartic release. ….I began to feel as if I was approaching my limit.'
'I am greatly bothered by my findings. I wonder what if anything can be done to validate my findings and even if so, what could be done to stop this.'

Well, while this may seem wildly outlandish and pure fiction to those who are not seers nor commune with spirits who give them visions and insights, back in 2008, the man who found the 5th foot did say to *The Guardian* newspaper that he suspected it was as a result of foul play.
"There's someone doing this all right. Think about it - if they tied a chain around someone's ankle and threw them overboard, the foot would pop off. That could explain it. Maybe they got a lot of bodies stored up in a container and they got washed out. We don't know. There's a lot of stuff goes on over there," he said, rather cryptically….

In a previous book I made reference to numerologist Ellis C Taylor who is explicit in his belief that not only does satanic ritual of the elite take place on ley energy lines of power, but that this is inextricably linked to the disappearance and deaths of missing children in the United Kingdom and worldwide.

He has identified 'patterns' in these 'abductions and murders' of children and teenagers over the last few decades which strongly tie in with important occult dates, numerology, and ley lines, he believes.

The path of travel in these abduction and murder cases, he believes, are via ley-lines which intersect ancient places of powerful black energy. His implication is that occult ritual sacrifice is being conducted to harness the black energy, with the use of abducted children and adults.

David Icke is a believer of this pattern-linking concept too, and will openly say that those who are secretly in control of us, the 'shape-shifting bloodline,' need this negative energy of fear and pain to feed off.

In one of Ellis Taylor's abduction/murder cases, that of a young boy Daniel Nolan, he believes that the black energy line runs from the Isle of Wight, crossing the ancient Stonehenge, and the Severn Bridge; a notorious bridge for suicides.

As outlandish as it sounds, do horrific abductions and murders serve to energise this 'grid?' Are the negative emotions and fears of the people in the area, knowing an abduction has taken place and desperately searching for the missing, deliberately caused by an occult cabal to create greater swathes of negative emotion to feed the 'grid' and those black practitioners that feed off of that grid?

Both Ellis and Ike assert that they do. Icke claims that from evidence he's directly received by a number of people heavily entrenched in ritual and the occult, of people that have attended and participated in the ritual killings of children in these ceremonies, this is for the purpose of harnessing greater powers of darkness to enable their ruling bloodline to continue and thrive.

Pure craziness, or is there something to it? -The abduction/murder case that Ellis refers to above is that of Daniel Nolan. Over on the mainland, across the seven-mile stretch of sea from the Isle of Wight, a teenage boy disappeared after night fishing with his friends. I bring this case up, because he was later found, or rather, one of his feet was later found, washed up on a beach.

It was early January 2002 when he disappeared. He'd been fishing with friends off the Hamble waterfront, near Southampton. Fourteen-year-old Daniel had fished many times before. It was his main hobby, along with swimming and he was a member of the Sea Scouts.

When he didn't come home in the early hours of the morning as he had promised, his mother began to get concerned, and after half an hour she went out herself to look for him, knowing where he would be.

She found only his fishing equipment. She called the police and by 4.30 in the morning a search had begun for him. Specialist sniffer dogs could pick up no scent of him. Five teams of police divers and two army sonar units could also detect no trace of him.

He'd left his friends at close to midnight, after they'd all finished fishing early and hung out up the street by the local shops. When they all decided to go home, he headed back to the waterfront to fetch his fishing gear and go home too.

Almost a year later, a lady was walking her dog in a scenic bay called Chapman's Pool near Swanage, in Dorset. An entirely different county and over forty miles away. She stumbled across a shocking sight. It was a human foot still in its shoe, washed up onto the beach.

After DNA forensic analysis found that it was part of Daniel's body, tidal experts were brought in to try to explain how the foot, still in the trainer and sock, had managed to travel 40 miles in the sea to this cove.

It was determined that his foot had come away as a natural process from his body, but speculation obviously grew that he could have been taken by someone in a vehicle, or onto a boat.

His parents at the time of his disappearance were so convinced he was still alive and being held somewhere that they put up a £50,000 reward, but it was never claimed.

The area in which his foot was discovered, though accessible to those local to the area if they had knowledge of it, and experience of climbing down into the bay, was not an easy nor simple path to take. It can be accessed though, and, perhaps crucially it can obviously also be accessed by boat, by simply dropping anchor further out in the bay.

Police at the time, after launching a massive ground, sea and air search, concluded that the boy had fallen in while night-fishing, and been swept out to sea.

Though he was under legal drinking age, he had consumed alcohol that night; however, as has been said, he was a Sea Scout, an active and highly competent swimmer, a canoeist, and very familiar with the sea tides in that area, where he grew up.

His Mother didn't find the police explanation acceptable. Talking at the time of the tragedy, she said, "This raises more questions than it answers. We must emphasize; this does not tell us the circumstances of his disappearance."

She spoke out on news programmes at the time, expressing concern that it could have been the result of foul play, calling it a 'strange and bizarre case.'

She simply doesn't believe that if he had fallen into the water, he could have been swept away so far.

"Anyone else who's fallen in the water in recent years there has always been able to be found."

Crucially, of the waterfront where he was fishing, she says, "It's in an *enclosed sheltered* waterway." Was he taken onto a boat? A yacht perhaps?

Not only do we have the 'visions' of the man who calls himself Papa Crocodile, the Palo Mayombe priest, but of course, David Ike exposed the alleged disposal of young boys from a Yacht owned by a former British Prime Minister (whose name is easily found online). It was Ike's assertion over a decade ago, that the former Prime Minister had gone for jaunts on a Yacht off the Jersey coast, with underage boys, and sexually assaulted them, then thrown them overboard, to drown.

While almost everyone mocked this assertion as ridiculous, in 2016, mainstream newspaper *The Daily Mail* published the story of a mother 'who claims she had told police a child vanished after going on ……'s yacht, but officers were warned not to investigate by 'someone above.'

Of course, Ike being the controversial figure that he is, has always been roundly criticised and ridiculed for his outrageous statements, such as his insistence that the Royal Family are 'reptilian.' So, it has always been very easy for the general public to pay no notice to any of the extreme things he comes out with. However, over the last few years, the topic of the former Prime Minister, and others in seats of power, has been harder to keep out of the public arena, most notably after the revelations of the Jimmy Saville paedophile crimes and his closeness to those in positions of power and wealth.

Then, the Daily Mail newspaper and others, began to publish articles in 2016 which covered the very same allegations. 'Mother Linda Corby claims 11 boys boarded the yacht (of the former Prime Minister) But only 10 returned. She claims she went to the police – who were told not to investigate.' "Perhaps he was dropped off somewhere," Corby says to the reporter, "But it was suspicious."

The Newspaper points out here, "Jersey is one of at least 7 police forces now investigating alleged abuse" at the hands of the former Prime Minister. Corby said she watched as the young boys all boarded the yacht but when it returned, only hours later, she counted only ten boys disembark and walk away.' The boys were aged between 6 to 11 years of age and had come from the children's home on the small Island, called Haute de la Garenne.

This children's home became the focus of a police investigation when it emerged in 2016 that up to 50 suspects had engaged in abusing the children who lived there. An active paedophile ring appeared to have been operating at the children's home for decades, some suspects of which the police said, "are people of pubic prominence." Wiltshire Chief Constable said a significant number of people had disclosed claims of historical abuse against the ex-prime minister.

The day Corby watched the Yacht pull away from the dock in Jersey, and later return, she claims she and Jersey senator Ralph Vibert, who has now died, were "warned" about ..... and then "watched in horror" as they saw one child was missing.

In 2015, Jersey police launched 'Operation Whistle,' to investigate child abuse claims and said they believed it involved "13 politicians, celebrities and sports stars." The then Prime Minister was one of them. However, it would seem that this investigation as well as others across several other police forces, came to nothing for some reason....

Former crewmates of the former prime minister however, accused police of dragging out a "ludicrous" investigation into claims he abused and murdered children on his yacht.

The *Daily Mail* quoted an officer 'who was at the heart of some of the most sensitive inquiries back in the 1990's,' who said; "I have no doubt that the allegation that a prosecution was stopped in suspicious circumstances, because of a potential link to ...., is true." In other words, he means it was hushed up. Which version is true?

The idea of feet washing up, detached from bodies, of children or adults vanishing, are they all "accidents" or "unexplained/unknown" or may indeed they have really sinister causes...?

Chapter 5: Monsters, Machines, and the Missing

In this chapter, we take a look at things in the sky, that may be related to people going missing. Are they monsters or machines? ……

When pilot Kenneth Arnold had his now-famous sighting of 'things' in the sky in the 1940's in Mount Rainier National Park, he estimated a wingspan at a minimum of 100 feet, flying close to the horizon toward Mount Rainer. For three minutes, he watched 'them' considering 'them' to be living organisms – "sort of like sky-jellyfish."

He had another sighting afterwards, in which he said he had seen up to 25 small "craft." In a third sighting in the sky above California in 1952 while flying his plane, he said he saw 2 craft, one of which he described as "solid as a car," while the other craft he said was "semi-transparent." This second craft was below his plane and he said that he could see through the craft to the trees below.

This led him to conclude that the objects he encountered in the sky possessed the ability to alter their density and that they were actually living cells of organisms.

"The impression I had after observing these strange objects was that they were something alive rather than machines. Living organisms of some sort, that has the ability to change its density, similar to jelly-fish. After years of extensive research my conclusion is that some of the so-called "unidentified flying objects" are not 'space ships' from another planet at all, but rather, are masses of living objects that are as much a part of Space as the life we find in the oceans."

One pilot told him that he was approached while in flight by what he called a "rayfish" that was larger than his airplane. The edges of its wings were reportedly described as behaving in a way like a sea ray, in that "it rippled."

Fifty years after these statements from Kenneth Arnold, a sighting was reported in Utah, in 2011. From an anonymous source, the account reads as such; "It was not too far above my home. It appeared to be a misty cloud, shaped like a boomerang/chevron. It was moving quickly across the sky East to West. It was almost transparent, and at first, I thought it was mist. However, it was a very clear night, and there was no wind, and so I realized that it could not be mist nor a cloud, because it didn't dissipate or change in shape, but it moved incredibly fast."

"It made no sounds. I tried to get a clearer look but it seemed transparent and it was moving so quick. I think it had white lights, but can't be sure. A plane that had been in the sky before this was much higher up in the sky and was still in the sky after this object had gone out of the range of my sight."

Several decades ago Navy veteran Trevor Constable believed, after dedicating twenty years to studying them, that morphic beasts lived in the sky and he could capture them on film with the use of infra-red cameras. He said that they were monsters that only increased their density while in search of food; their food source being humans. He blamed the accounts of livestock disappearances on these soaring predatory entities, as well as the constant stream of people going missing every year in forests and the wilderness.

The Muskegon Chronicle of May 21, 1998 wrote of a strange incident in the Minastee National Forest, when school children and their accompanying teachers were witness to a large silent object, described as shaped like a 'protozoa or omeba,' which appeared to float slowly over the tree-line above them.

The body of the object was described as being 'like shimmering gossamer,' and 'almost transparent or insubstantial' yet it also seemed to be illuminated by lights.

The 'Mundrabilla Incident,' in Australia, 1988, received national coverage at the time. In 1988, a mother and her three adult sons were forced to drive desperately through the desert highway of the Nullarbor Plain, southern Australia late one night, after a huge glowing object landed hard on the roof of their car. With it came the most "foul smell" described by them as "like rotting decomposing flesh of dead bodies,"

At one point, the mother said she reached her arm out the car window and grasped hold of it, touching the 'body,' which she later said felt "spongy." Their dogs in the car were going crazy. When she brought her hand back inside the car she saw it was covered in a dark dust.

The family became disoriented and felt that their voices had become slower, and lower in pitch. They believed at this point that they were going to die. One of the adult sons, Patrick said that he felt that his 'brain was being sucked out', and Mrs Knowles likened it to having something 'going into our heads'. Then, whatever it was apparently suddenly lifted the entire car up off the ground.

Not long after, it fortunately also dropped the car, causing one of their tyres to pop. The family left the car hurriedly and hid in some bushes by the side of the road. They remained there for 15 minutes before changing the tyre and continuing on to the nearest town.

At the same time, a truck driver called Mr Graham Henley had also seen the strange object, and described it as being like a "big fried egg, hung upside down." He also confirmed there was black ash on the family's car, having witnessed the family's desperate encounter. He, as well as the police, later confirmed the indents found in the family's car had been caused by "something" landing on the roof.

Cryptozoologist Ivan T Sanderson proposed the same idea as Trevor Constable and Kenneth Arnold, that huge entities lived in the sky. He, as well as Fortean Charles Fort also both investigated the "The Crawford Monster" incident in Indiana, way back in 1891, when a monster seemed to come from the sky.

The *Indiana Journal* in September 1891, as well as the *Brooklyn Eagle* newspaper first covered this, and contemporary journalist, Vincent P. Gaddis, in his book "Mysterious fires and lights." Of the Crawford incident, Gaddis wrote; "All point to this 'object' being a living thing, one of the hypothetical atmospheric life-forms of UFO's."

The first sighting was at 2 a.m. on September 4th, 1891, when an object was seen circling a house before flying away to the East, and then returning some time later before flying out of sight. Two days later, on September 6th, it flew over the Town with 100 witnesses. The description of the object was that it had glowing red eyes, was a large rectangular shape, eel- like, and undulating with fins. It was 'writhing' or 'squirming' as it moved, and made a "wheezing sound."

Two days after this sighting, two men saw it, and this time according to fortean Charles Fort they described it as 'a seemingly headless monster, or a 'construction' approximately 20 feet long and 8 feet wide. It was moving across the sky seemingly propelled by fin-like attachments. It moved toward the men. The men moved. It sailed off, but made such a noise that Methodist Pastor Reverend G. Switzer was awoken by it and looking out from his window saw the object circling the sky.'

Charles Fort says he thought there would be no Mr. Switzer when he read about the sightings and decided to investigate, thinking it had to be a hoax, but he was surprised that he did indeed find a Reverend Switzer living in the area, and he stood by his testimony.

Fort continues; 'Brooklyn, September 1877, a Mr. W.H. Smith saw a winged human form.' In Chile too, in 1868, 'a construction that carried lights and was propelled by a noisy motor or a gigantic bird, eyes wide open and shinning like burning coals covered with immense scales, which clashed together with a metallic sound.'

In June 1873, in Bonham, Texas, a farmer called Mr. Hardin, saw an enormous flying snake, a silvery serpent, with brilliant yellow stripes twisting in the sky. Then other witnesses came forward too. Cotton field workers saw it in the sky above them, causing them to run in panic for cover. The local newspaper *The Enterprise* published accounts of witnesses who saw it coil itself up and then thrust its enormous head as though striking out at something.

The *New York Times* took the opinion that the sightings at this time were due to drinking and suggested the accounts were from witnesses suffering from "delirium tremens." The object apparently circled the town but was going at such speed that it became a blur. Twenty-four hours after this, an object fitting this description was seen in Kansas. It caused the same panic. This time, it was soldiers at Fort Scott who fled the open ground.

Dr Tom Scott, former curator of Fannin County Museum of History wrote about the strange reports in the Bonham skies. "In March 1897, a cigar shaped object was reported and that same month, the *Dallas News* and others reported similar sightings. A farmer said he was chased by the object that was dragging an anchor along the ground. The farmer said the anchor snagged his pants and raised him into the air until his pants ripped and he fell.'

Two weeks later, a man traveling between Bonham and Denison also said he saw "some kind of manufactured craft." Other witnesses who said they also had seen it, said it was of a length estimated at "200 feet long, with large windows." Some people even said they "heard hymns being sung as it passed overhead."

According to fortean Jerome Clark, in May 1888 in North Carolina, three sisters out walking in the woods saw a hissing 15-foot serpent sailing above the tree tops, moving at the speed of a hawk. Other local people also saw it, according to the *New York Times.*

In 1897, two decades after 'the Crawford Monster,' sightings, the *Charleston News and Courier* mentioned the most recent sighting of "the flying snake." It was sighted twice on 11 July near Newman Swamp, 10 miles south of Hartsville, at six and seven o'clock, though the newspaper writer neglects to inform us if that's am or pm.

The second witness, identified as Henry Polson, was quoted as saying; "The monster was low down, just above the tree top. It had its head thrown back in a position to strike and was just floating through the atmosphere lengthwise." It was anywhere from twenty-five feet to forty feet in length.

According to research by Chad Arment, 'Pterodactyls' were seen in Selma, California in the 1880's. In 1882, chickens were found eaten with "huge teeth marks" which could have been the result of very large dogs, or, something else.

Two hog farmers near Selma saw the creatures under a bridge. A posse was put together for an all-night vigil in an attempt to capture or kill the monsters, but they had no luck. In the morning, ducks were found ripped apart and eaten on a near-by farm. The next night two of the men, JD Daniels and a Mr Templeton, dug holes to hide in near the water.

The cries were heard in the direction of a river, approximately 4 miles away. The ominous yells drew nearer. Then suddenly they heard the rush of wings. The two 'dragons' came swooping down "so hideous that our hair almost stood on end. The two creatures circled round and round the pond in rapid whirls, screaming hideously all the while. Their eyes were plainly visible.

Instead of bills like birds, they had snouts like alligators and their teeth could be seen as they snapped their jaws. "They came down with a fearful plunge into the pond and the water flew as though a tree had fallen. They dived around in the water, wings folded on their backs. Their eyes seemed all the while wide open and staring." The two men shot at them, one flew off injured and the other crawled out of the water, and dragged itself across the field but was too fast for the men to catch.

So, going back over 100 years, we have the dichotomy of sightings of both strange sky serpents, and also, of what appear to be 'manufactured' crafts. On April 27th, 2012, a lady called Heather, who lives in great Barrington, Massachusetts, filmed the sky from her car as she was driving along in a semi-suburban area. With her phone camera tilting up toward the sky, the tops of roofs and tree tops were visible.

On arriving home, she then examined the camera footage, and began to make notes of her observations. She says that strange things have been appearing in the skies where she lives, for some time now. On this occasion, she comments that there was thick low cloud coverage of about 99%, with solid white over

almost the entire sky. It was as she reviewed the footage at home that she says, "Watch what happens….right there in the middle. Watch the middle of the screen…there it goes!…"
On the footage, a weird large but narrow horizontal rectangular object appears amid the very thick solid white clouds. It looks like a wide rectangular box. Which very bizarrely then goes downward and backwards back into the cloud! It very much looks like you're watching a CGI or computer-generated image or some kind of movie special effect. The clouds are low to the ground. The white framed box goes down and back into the thick cloud as though pulled by something, and yet this does not appear to be an altered image or tampered-with footage. The car is moving past trees and houses.

She says, as the footage is replayed more slowly again, "It begins rod-like," and it does, as a long white line, like a white horizontal pole appears in front of the thick clouds. It appears solid, rigid, and we're not talking about amorphous, fibrous amoeba natural beings here; this looks artificial. It looks like an artificial box. There's also a strange blue emanation in the clouds near-by.

"I've seen many bizarre things here in the sky," Heather says, bemused and indeed quite alarmed. The rod-like thing in the clouds changes suddenly into a long narrow horizontal rectangle "with bad teeth" as Heather describes it, and while that does sound immensely comical, it does almost appear as though this "machine" has a row of "teeth" now! Not because it appears like a Sky-beast or Atmospheric-being, but rather, it looks like a machine in the sky!

Brightening screen contrast can help see the image more, and Heather says, "This no doubt helps one's ability to see what clearly was not meant to be seen. Frankly, it scared me. It's like...I don't know. Anybody? What could it possibly be?! You can see a shadow of this.....this is Nano-technology....these clouds put on a "performance" for me. I don't even tell anyone about this – what can I tell them?! It's so overwhelming I don't even know where to begin."

Best guesses from commentators on her video suggest, "Project blue beam?" And "Haarp toys for the Government." Others say it's a "Morning Glory cloud;" a rare but meteorological normality consisting of a low-level atmospheric solitary wave and associated cloud, occasionally observed in different locations around the world. The wave often occurs as an amplitude-ordered series of waves forming bands of roll clouds. Others on seeing it do however call it a "Machine in the sky...."

Going from Machines back to Monsters, we now have the strange case of number 68439 in the MUFON case book. It's an image of a dark brown/black object with what looks like a long two-pronged tail, entering the clouds. It was taken on July 30th, 2015 at 7.56 p.m. It looks like the tail end of either an enormous (and physically impossibly-sized) swallow, or some type of unidentified but rather sinister-looking creature, which some have said looks like it comes from hell. It appears to be a giant dark beast with a solid, square body. Only the lower end of the body is visible, the rest is hidden by the low-lying cloud into which it appears to have flown up into.

When the picture began to circulate, most reports called it "eerie" "creepy" and "satanic." The witness took it in El Paso, Texas. "I was taking photographs of the clouds as the sun was setting and I caught something else by accident. It wasn't some big event; it was an accidental picture but of something really strange. I didn't notice until later when I showed my wife what I thought were some great photos I took of the sun set. I took pictures before and it was not there. There were no birds around – there's no trees this side of town. Then I came across this picture and am baffled as to what it could be. What is this strange appearance in the sky?"

The man's critics pointed out that it was obviously a bird, such as a swallow, and perhaps it could be, yet the scale of the clouds are clear to see and it appears to be absolutely huge. Impossible to be a bird against the clouds and so the only other option would that it would have to be photoshopped. In these days of photo-trickery, perhaps it is faked and yet it does not appear to look like a hoax.

It looks extremely chilling. Is there a logical explanation for this enormous flying monster? Or, is it some kind of inter-dimensional or supernatural being? Many have said that it looks like Mothman....or worse.

According to writer Peter Haining, of 'Mammoth book of Hauntings,' in Runcorn, an ancient parish in the Liverpool area of the U.K., newspapers reported on a mystery "Thing" which was going on a murderous spree at a remote farm in 1953.

At a rural and remote 15th Century farm, animals were being found dead. Specifically, pedigree pigs which were being bred by farmer Mr. Crowther and his wife. More than fifty had been found dead, over a number of days, and yet despite the assessment of several veterinarians, none of them could find the cause for the deaths of the pedigree animals.

It had been happening for two weeks and each morning, pigs were found dead by the farmers, yet with no obvious reason to explain why or how they had died, and confounding the vets who attended the scene, carried out tests, and took specimens for analysis. All were dumbfounded as to what was happening, and it was indeed a mystery, as the pigs would always appear fine and fit when the farmers last saw them on their evening rounds before retiring to bed.

When interviewed, after it finally stopped, the farmer told the newspapers, "After the last one died, I saw a large black cloud, about seven feet in height. It was shapeless apart from there were two prongs poking out at the back and moving. This shapeless mass approached me, stopping at about five feet from me. Then it turned in the direction of the pig sty and went in there."

His wife had just as terrifying and inexplicable an experience with this "black mass." "It was smaller and wider. It was like smoke being drawn by suction."
What on earth was this thing? Where did it come from? And how was it killing the animals?

In perhaps a less sinister but just as baffling tale, from '*True ghost stories of the british isles*,' J. P. J. Chapman tells a very strange story. "Many years ago, my late father-in-law rented a large farm near Bampton in Devon. The farm buildings and the farm house were situated half-way up a steep hill which overlooked the River Exe. During a warm summer it was nice, but there was a lingering threat of bitter winds and snow in the winters.

There was a lane going from the farm land to a large moor, which was 300 feet higher than the fields. Now, it is well known that large open spaces, devoid of useful vegetation and situated at the top of a high hill frequently possess a bad reputation.

On summer evenings, my wife and I frequently took walks to the moor. It commanded a wonderful view, while the sunsets were a sight to behold. The land ended at a gate which led onto the moor. Quite a while before the events to be related, my wife and I often remarked that it was an eerie spot and the sooner we passed it the better. Personally, I never gave it much thought, being a "country lad" - I knew of many such places that were not nice, and that was all to be said about it. However, things were to prove otherwise.

My wife and her sisters rode a lot and they took turns to exercise the horses. Sometimes they went out together. On one occasion, one of the sisters was asked by her father to go on the moor to see if some cattle had strayed. It was autumn and, the sun having already set, it would soon be dark. The girl rode up alone, and having seen that all was well with the cows, she was just about to leave the moor through the gate she had left open, when the horse suddenly shied. Nothing would induce it to pass through the gate. There was no alternative route except by a long detour, so they had to go through.

After several attempts, she decided to dismount and lead the horse through. This time as they reached the gate a curious luminous shape could be seen drifting nearby. It was "like an elongated sausage, with baleful eyes." The whole thing seemed to be pulsating, from dim to bright. It was in a vertical position except for a sideways, wavering movement. The girl was frightened, to say the least, but she made her mind up to face it. Placing herself between whatever it was and the horse, she coaxed the horse through. When the horse was half-way it broke loose and galloped away down the lane.

There were several curious facts about this- it seemed that it only took place at dusk - no other time. No other animals except horses – any horse – were affected. But – it had to be both horse and human. If there was not this combination, then nothing happened. The "Ghost sausage" as it was dubbed, seemed anchored in one spot, its movements restricted as such. Several times I visited the place but while noticing that there was something there, could never decide what. There was a big disused quarry nearby; perhaps some earth spirit had been released. It was greenish in colour and about a foot wide and five feet in height.

On the subject of more fully-formed monsters; The 'Flatwoods Monster' is somewhat akin to the Mothman. It was reputedly a monster that terrified and traumatised a group of both children and adults in the Flatwoods area of West Virginia, in September 1952.

This group of children and adults were all out in the night-time in the Flatwoods because they had seen what they thought was either a meteor or a 'UFO' landing on the top of a near-by hill there, and they intent on going to find out what had happened.

The incident appeared to begin early in the evening, after sunset, when brothers Fred, 13 and Edward May, 12, along with their younger friend Tommy Hyer, saw a bright object in the sky, moving across it before appearing to come down in a nearby field owned by local farmer Mr. G. Fisher.

The boys ran home and told their mom what they had just seen. They told her they had seen a UFO land in the farmer's field. Their mother, Kathleen Hill, accompanied by a national guardsman called Eugene Lemon, all went quickly on foot toward the spot the boys said the craft had landed.

The guardsman's dog also accompanied them, and as dogs do, it ran ahead of them and reached the spot before the group did. However, the dog returned very quickly to the group, whimpering with its tail between its legs, clearly frightened. As the group on foot reached the top of the hill where the boys said the craft had landed, they all later testified that they discovered an object amid a glowing pulsing ball of "fire." In the air, there was also a mist and a strong odour that they said burnt their eyes and noses.

It was the national guardsman who then also spotted something else. He saw two small lights by the side of the large glowing object. Shining his flashlight over at them, he saw something that caused his heart to pound. Underneath a large low-hanging tree where the small lights were, was a monster. It moved, and began coming toward him and the rest of the group, bounding toward them and from it came a shrill noise. It appeared to glide, or float, but then veered off and went toward the fire-ball.

According to the mother, Kathleen Hill, the monster was at least 10-feet-tall, and she believed it appeared to be wearing a long cloak with a hood over its head, like a monk. Its face however, was definitely not human. She described it as a round shape and with blood-red with eyes that bulged out and glowed an orange hue. They all fled in absolute terror. Almost all of them afterward were deemed to be incoherent with hysteria and shock, and vomiting.

The boy's mother contacted the Sheriff once they were home, and the Sheriff, Robert Carr carried out questioning to find out what they said had happened up on the hill. He also went to the scene of the alleged incident accompanied by the national guard. The awful odour still permeated the air but there was no monster now nor any craft or fire.

The local newspapers went to the scene the next day; but nothing of the strange orb or the monstrous creature remained. All that was left were some strange tracks in the grass, and a strange unfamiliar smell. Local Newspaper owner Mr. A. Stewart went to the site the next morning, and saw strange tracks in the mud as well as an unidentified black thick liquid on the ground. The tracks however were later assumed by some to have been caused by a pick-up truck of an inquisitive person who had also gone to look for the monster and the craft.

Interestingly, paranormal investigators a Mr. William and Ms. Smith, who belonged to the 'Civilian Saucer Investigation' group based in Los Angeles, says they interviewed a woman in her early twenties and her mother, who reported to them a very similar experience. They claimed to have had an encounter with a monster of the same appearance and accompanied by the same dreadful odour, a few days before the Flatwoods incident.

It would also appear that the young woman had to be hospitalized for 21 days due to an undefined sickness. The original group who had their encounter on the hill, were reported as suffering from sickness too; particularly the guardsman, who suffered ongoing breathing problems and severe continued vomiting. The others of the group also suffered swelling of their throats and difficulty swallowing. The Newspapers of the day reported the encounter with the entity on the hill as "a ten-foot Frankenstein-like monster," however, they added, "State Police laughed off the reports as hysteria. They said the so-called monster had grown from 7 feet to 17 feet in 24 hours."

The guardsman however, stuck to his account that he saw a pair of bright eyes, a creature of ten feet in height, with a "blood red face." The Newspaper owner who interviewed them said, "These people were the most scared people I've ever seen. People don't make up that kind of story." "It looked worse than Frankenstein," the boy's mother said.

Most bizarre of all, one of the boys described the appearance of the monster as having "a head which resembled the ace of spades, and clothing which from the waist down, hung in great folds."

Sceptics have said it was nothing more than a large owl. For the witnesses, this was an impossibility to even begin to agree with. Even more curiously, on a forum discussing this 'monster,' are two very similar accounts, but with a wholly different interpretation....

Chapter 6: The 'Brujas.'

While discussing the Flatwoods Monster, this account came about;

"I have a little story to tell you guys. I once made a t-shirt with a print of the drawing of the flatwood monster. This was 8 years ago when I was living in Albuquerque. One day I was wearing the t-shirt in a local supermarket when this Mexican dude came and asked me about the drawing in the t-shirt. He asked what it was because he said that it looked a lot like the "brujas" in his home town of Rayones in Mexico.

I asked what a "bruja" was and he said witches. He told me that in his home town near the mountains you can see fire balls floating on the top of the mountains and that a few of the people that lived near the mountain have seen the witches, including him, and they look just like the thing I had on my t-shirt. I did a bit of research on this and the home town of this guy is located near a place called Monterrey, where a police officer was on the News because he reported being attacked by a Witch that he reported to be very tall, with red eyes, a pointy hood-like figure on its head and slender arms with claws. There's even some footage of one of those things flying around Monterrey City. Interesting how similar those two beings are from two different locations - Monterrey and Flatwoods."

I found another similar account, in a different forum. "I have something really weird for y'all. This past December in Mexico it was like near 3.a.m. and I was outside around a fire keeping ourselves warm with my younger brother and my four cousins. We were just talking when we started to hear dogs barking and crying and the cows nearby started making weird noises too.

 We didn't really worry about it, but then two red balls came out from the side of a hill. My cousin said; "It's ok; they're tractors." I asked him, "Why would there be tractors over there at 3 a.m.?" Then we remembered that our aunt had warned me not to go near there at night supposedly because the Brujas (Witches) come out. I started laughing when she told me that because it sounded so stupid to me. Well, then my younger brother says, what if they are Brujas and we all stop talking. Then my cousin says, "What if they see the fire...?" And we all take off running into the house because we see one of the red balls getting closer.

We get inside and close the door. We were like "Wtf was that...?" And then all of sudden someone or something is trying to open the door violently. My little brother runs to my mom's room and tells her. She comes out and the door is still trying to get open. Then my mom walks towards the door and it goes away.

Next day we went to the hill to see what was there... and there was this black doll standing up. I never went back to that hill after that. We saw many red balls during those two weeks in Mexico. They would move back and forth and back and forth...it was crazy... I also a UFO. Oh...and one night when I was outside I was closing the gate and someone was saying my name close to my ear (But I was by myself!!) It sounded like a girl's voice...I don't know if y'all are going to believe me because it sounds stupid but man, I take it serious now.'

Chapter 7: Death & the Skin Walkers

Before we get to the unexplained deaths, there was this strange story, given by Navajo_Joe; 'I was a kid when this happened. My uncle and I were finishing up gathering firewood because it was getting dark. Driving back on the dirt road I had this awful sense of being watched.

Before I could turn to look out my passenger window, my uncle shouted; "Don't!" I froze. I heard a 'tap-tap' on my window. My heart felt like it was beating out of my chest. My uncle sped up and began praying in my native language. I didn't know what was going on, but I thought it was all over – until our truck suddenly dipped.

My uncle began saying; "Look at me! Don't turn away!" over and over again. Then I heard it again; 'tap-tap,' but this time it was coming from the window behind me! It was getting harder for me to breathe. I wanted to cry.

A minute or so passed and the truck dipped again. My uncle looked around and sighed. It was quiet. "We will ask your father to do a prayer so the evil will forget our faces," he said. I remember curling up on the seat and just staring, my uncle singing an old prayer until we got home.'

In 2005, a post appeared on SG Forum. It described the experience of a young lady. All of her life, Frances T. says she has seen things, and heard things. She was born into a family of sensitives, and accepted that this was 'normal' for her. However, nothing could have prepared her for what they encountered one dark night on a remote and desolate road in Arizona 20 years ago.

The family had moved to Flagstaff, Arizona in 1978 shortly after she had graduated high school. Not long after this, the family decided to go on a road trip back to their home county in Wyoming in the family pickup truck, to visit friends.

Route 163 took them through the Monument Valley Navajo Tribal Park on the Navajo Reservation. "My friend, a Navajo, warned us of traveling through the reservation, especially at night."

The trip was uneventful. But their return journey more than justified the warning. "To this day, I have major anxiety attacks when I have to travel through the north country at night. I avoid it at all costs."

It was about 10:00 p.m. that night when the family were heading back. It was a long stretch of road and so pitch black they could only see a few feet beyond the headlights on that moonless night.

Her father was driving, with she and her mom in the cab beside him and her brother in the back of the pickup. Suddenly, her father broke the silence. "We have company."

She and her mom turned to look out the back window. Headlights appeared over the crest of a hill, then disappeared as the car went down, then reappeared. Thunder began in the distance and her father decided her brother should come inside. She opened the slider window and her brother crawled in. The car was still behind them.

She watched as the car's headlights crest another hill. It didn't reappear. She kept watching, turning every couple of minutes but never saw them reappear.

When she turned one last time, the truck was rounding a tight corner in the road, and her father slowed the truck. From that moment, the atmosphere changed somehow. Time itself almost seemed to stop.

Her mother screamed, while her father cried out "Jesus! What the hell is that!?"

She had no idea what was happening. Her brother was now yelling "What is it? What is it?" Her father immediately flipped on the inside light, and she could see he was petrified. "I have never seen my father that scared in my life. He was white as a sheet."

Panic was filling the cab. Her mother was wringing her hands. Her brother just kept saying "Oh my God! Oh my God!"

As the pickup sped round the corner, her father hit the brakes to stop the truck from going into the ditch. Something leaped out of the ditch. It was black, hairy and was at eye-level to them. If it was a man it was like no man she had ever seen.

Despite its monstrous appearance, whatever it was, it wore man's clothes. "It had a blue and white checked shirt and I think jeans. Its arms were raised up over its head. Its eyes were yellow and its mouth was open."

Although time seemed frozen in this moment of horror, it was over within a few minutes as the cab raced away from the thing. The car that had been following them never did show up. They drove all the way home with the interior lights on.

However, that was not the end of it. Just a couple of nights later, she and her brother were woken by what sounded like drumming. Quickly they looked out the bedroom window into their backyard, which was surrounded by a tall fence and forest behind it. At first, they saw nothing but the forest. Then the sound of drumming got louder, and they saw a group of "men" appear behind the fence. It looked like they were trying to scale the fence to climb over, but they couldn't manage to climb it as it was so high. They began to chant.

A few days later she asked a Navajo friend about that strange and frightening night. The friend told her it was a Skinwalker that night on the road and she added that that the 'men' who had come to her house and began chanting had been skinwalkers too, and that they wanted her family, but could not gain access because something was protecting them.

"Your family has a lot of power," the Navajo friend said, "and they wanted it."

In June 1987, in a rocky and wooded hillside area behind a medical centre in Flagstaff, Arizona, the body of a mutilated woman was found, sparking one of the strangest criminal cases in history.

The body of a 40-year-old Navajo woman was found by concerned co-workers out looking for her. She was naked and had sustained numerous stab wounds to her upper body. Her left breast had been partially bitten off. Her face was battered and bruised so badly that she was hardly recognisable.

She was later confirmed to be the missing housekeeper of the medical centre close-by and she had been working the night-shift before she had vanished. Her name was Sarah Saganitso and she left behind a 4-year-old son. It had been the first time she had worked the night-shift. Her co-workers had been searching for her after her car was found still in the medical centre car park but there had been no sign of her.

The local Flagstaff newspaper, The Courier, reported on the discovery of her body, describing her as suffering a "violent death." Her body had been found "between rock crevices on a wooded hillside," said police spokesman Robert White.

She had worked at the medical centre for over 15 years. Co-worker and friend Helen Jaramillo, who was a cook at the medical centre, was the one who stumbled across the shocking sight of her friend's naked and bloodied body. She said that the only way she could tell it was her friend, was from her hair.

The newspaper quoted police reports as saying that the victim had last been seen Friday by a caretaker of the centre at approximately 10.55 pm, five minutes before the end of her shift. Friends and relatives had begun looking for her when she had not arrived home to care for her small son. By 11.30 a.m. the next morning, a missing person's report had been filed with the police.

Jaramillo said that her car was still in the car park and she couldn't understand why she would have been walking west of the medical centre, in the direction her body was found. "The first thing I wondered was whether it was someone who knew her pretty well and if that person also took her out of the building," she told the *Arizona Republic*. "It's very poorly lit on the west side of the building." Her friend said that after receiving some training classes, the murdered woman had been newly assigned to the late shift and that this had been her first one.

Police Sergeant Pascal Macias said that she had suffered lacerations, "made by a sharp instrument believed to be a knife." Autopsy reports indicated that she had died of suffocation however, although Macias said that the exact method of this had not been determined.

Three months later, a suspect was arrested for the killing. Former Northern Arizona University Teacher, George W. Abney M.A., 36, was being held in the county jail without a bond, after he had confessed to police that he was the killer. This stunned his former students and teachers alike.

He had first apparently confessed to killing the hospital worker in a phone call he placed from his mother's house to his pastor at the church he attended. Reverend Floyd Patterson of the Flagstaff Tabernacle Church later testified that Abney, a member of his congregation, had told him he had dreamt of the killing and was having trouble sorting out reality from his dreams.

Prior to this, police sergeant Macias said the teacher "had made statements in regard to the murder." A friend of the teacher said he had claimed to have dreamt about the murder, *before* it had happened. The man, who wished to remain anonymous for fear of his own safety, told the newspaper, he had been friends with the Teacher for 18 months and that he and another friend called George Bellas, were with the teacher at the time the woman was said to have been murdered. He said that when he had told police this, they had accused him of lying and of trying to protect his friend, the teacher. The man said that police told him that the teacher had already confessed.

His friend said he didn't know if the teacher had confessed but believed that he was being rail-roaded into confessing to something he didn't do and that they were acting like "head-hunters" and had arrested him just to have someone in custody for it. He said that his friend couldn't have done it; he and Bellas were with him, and that he was a quiet, intelligent and controlled person. "He never lost his temper. If something happened, he could figure it out. If you needed help; he'd help you. He was very quiet. There's no way he did it."

He added that the former teacher was stressed about school and work, and that perhaps his dreams had caused him to become confused. He said that Abney had told his friend Bellas that he'd been having dreams of the murder happening before it had happened. His friend now worried that this had made him think he had done it and had confessed to doing it.

His minister, Floyd Patterson said he believed that the teacher had had prophetic dreams "inspired by God." He said that Abney had predicated events in other people's lives too.

Students he had taught offered varying opinions about their teacher. Newspapers quoted anonymous students as saying their teacher was "a strange character" and "a little strange," with one student relating to the *Arizona Sun* Newspaper how "he was a fairly good teacher but he told strange stories about his childhood during class," although the student didn't elaborate further about the nature of these stories.

Head of his English department at the university, Dr Paul Ferlazzo said, "He was a serious and conscientious teacher. He was a quiet person." He added that the charges laid against the teacher had made everyone "very surprised and shocked," and many acquaintances of the teacher interviewed said they simply didn't believe him capable of murder.

In July 1988, one year later, the jury at the Coconino County Superior Court found Abney innocent of the 1st degree murder of Sarah Saganitso. The jury had deliberated for about four hours, considering the prosecution's argument that teeth marks found on the deceased woman's breast matched the teacher's teeth.

Now this is where it gets stranger. The jury also considered a highly unusual defence argument. The defence argued that because her body had been found with a broken stick laying over her neck and a clump of grass and earth had been placed beside her truck, which was traced back to the cemetery, then the murderer, the defence insisted, rather than being the teacher, could in fact be a skin walker.

They also argued that it could have been her former boyfriend, perhaps indicating they believed he was the 'skin walker' because he was Navajo and his alibi was that he had been in a sweat lodge at the time of her murder.

This defence, that a skin walker had killed her, was taken very seriously and given full consideration by the jurors. The teacher was acquitted.

On his not guilty verdict, the victim's sister, Rosemarie Williams, 33, said she "has no doubt about his innocence," and stated that she believed the killer was certainly still at large. Her husband too told the *Prescott Courier* that he believed the teacher was innocent and added that he now considered the teacher a friend. The teacher thanked the victim's family for their "prayful support."

As for the police, they still believed the teacher was the killer, while the defence stuck to their explanation that a skin walker had been responsible. It's believed to have been one of the very few times a skin walker has been offered as a suspect in a court of law.

A contact of mine however, Tony, pointed out to me that there may be more going on than a potential skin walker. "Three unsolved murder cases (including the one just discussed) occurred in Coconino County. Two of the cases took place 16 years apart; one in 1987 (Douglass Goss) and one in 2003 (Devil Dog Doe) She has never been identified. Both victims were beaten to death and dumped in Williams, Arizona, on a road by the name of Devil Dog Road. Efforts to identify the Devil Dog Jane Doe have included numerous interactions with law enforcement agencies, both nationally and internationally."

The first case, my contact Tony explained, was that of Douglas Goss, 28, who left his brother a note saying he was going to find a way to get from Guerneville, California, to his mother's house in Glendale, Arizona, in August 1987.

Coconino County Sheriff's Office deputies found his body in the forest just off Devil Dog Road near Williams on August 30th. He was killed by a blow to the head with a blunt object. His killer is still unknown.

Unemployed Goss was staying with his brother for two weeks, and then his brother was going to drive him to their mother's house in Glendale, Arizona. Instead of waiting on his brother however, Goss decided to leave a note on August 16th, saying he would find a way to get there on his own. He never arrived. His brother filed a missing-person report on September 11th.

He did not know that County deputies had found a body with no identification in the forest just off Devil Dog Road near Williams on August 30th. The body was of a man who had been killed with a blunt instrument to the head. The body was identified as being Goss in mid-December.
"The initial injury and the theft of his suitcase is unique," said Joe Sumner, volunteer investigator for the Coconino County Sheriff's Office cold case unit. Sumner, who retired from the National Park Service in 2007 as a criminal investigator, came

onto the cold case unit in 2008. Goss's body was decomposed and found 200 yards south of Interstate 40, and about 150 feet off Devil Dog Road. His approximate death was August 18th, just 48 hours after he left his brother.

Devil Dog Road was the location for another dead body in October 2003 (as my contact John Stone points out) This time it was a female, whose body was laid to rest in Potter's Field, after it was unable to be identified. Her murder too remains unsolved. Her grave lies unmarked. She had also been hit on the head and her body dumped there, without clothes or i.d. Hunters, out on the first day of deer hunting season, found her body about 200 yards from their camp.

'Devil Dog Doe' as she was nicknamed, had lots of dental work done prior to her death, estimated to have cost around $20,000 at the time, and she had beautifully manicured nails. Her body was found with a bite mark on her right arm. (Perhaps reminiscent then of the bitten breast of the "skin walker" victim Sarah Saganitso.) Advances in DNA could apparently now make it possible to distinguish who made the bite, and if this is the case, then presumably the police have done this and the killer's DNA is not currently held in any police database? – which would mean the person has never been arrested yet for any criminal behviour?

Hunters discovered her body, which had been there from anywhere between a couple of days to two weeks, after one of them fired a shot at a deer and came upon her body in the wooded area. Drag marks at the scene indicated her body had been pulled along the ground for approximately 70 feet. She had received a fatal blow to her head and had been left face down. As there was little blood at the scene it indicated she had been most likely killed elsewhere according to the FBI.

She had eaten approximately 3 hours before her death and had been dead around 3 days. She was aged between 45-65 years old. Who was she?

Chapter 8: More go Missing

The search for Peter Jackson was stepped down from a full-scale search to 'limited continuous' status after incoming inclement weather was forecast. It was October 2nd, 2016 in Yosemite National Park and active searching for the missing man had now been called to a halt. 'Limited Continuous' meant that the 'field' search had now stopped but that any clues or information that came in, regarding the whereabouts of the missing man would be followed up on.

74-year-old Mr Jackson had sent a text to his son on the 17th of September, telling his son that he was en-route to the national park. His vehicle was later found at White Wolf campsite and it was discovered that he'd paid for his camping up until the 21st of September.

It is believed that he had gone on a day hike from the campsite, but had never returned back at the camp. It is not known what trail he took, although it was believed that he usually undertook hikes rated as 'moderate to strenuous' usually within a 5-mile length. Despite his older age, he was in peak physical condition and fitness, with no medical conditions.

He is still missing, after no evidence was found that could indicate where he'd gone or where his body was now.

From National Park service records, the search for Alexander Sevier was also changed from active to 'limited continuous,' after searches had failed to find him too. He was listed as missing after failing to return from a day hike in Yosemite in June 2017. He was also very physically fit, and a frequent solo hiker.

Sevier, 24, is active duty Navy. He was last seen at Housekeeping Camp at the beginning of May. The National park service were appealing for any witnesses who may have seen him in the area since then.

Search efforts were listed as comprising of Rangers looking on all popular hiking trails, trained dogs, 'YODOGS,' as wells as a helicopter and civilian volunteers. It's known that he'd spent the previous few days hiking around the Valley area of the National Park on his own, with no harm. His disappearance, like Peter Jackson's is a mystery.

Floyd E. Roberts III went missing inside Grand Canyon National Park, in June 2016. The 52-year-old Caucasian male was last seen, according to the National Park Service, wearing a red long-sleeved shirt and jeans, and carrying a backpack and a daypack.

According to the National Park Service, he became separated from his friends at approximately 4:45 pm, during an extremely hot day during a hike in a remote part of the Grand Canyon, on the Shivwits Plateau. This day's hike had been one of a series of planned hikes over the course of their 9-day planned trip.

Following an intensive 6-day search effort, the park service says, "the incident remains unresolved; the search for Roberts is in continuous, limited mode, in which rangers and pilots will continue to search for clues when in the area, with no additional clues to guide search efforts."

"On Friday, high school teacher Mr Roberts was with friends and family when he went missing on day 1 of their trip."

His friend Ned Bryant reported him missing to the National Park Service. They'd set out together, along with Bryant's daughter Madeleine, for another trip through the canyon. The group had reached a trail head on a hill when they decided to split up and take different routes. He and his daughter went one way and the school teacher went another way.

"I am very worried," Bryant wrote to his wife, Heidi Bryant, on Facebook. "Everything was going perfectly until the split. Helicopters, all afternoon couldn't find him."

He is still missing.

Chapter 9: Creepy Encounters in the woods

This account comes from a Park Ranger. "I and another Ranger were out on a search and rescue once. The missing person was a man in his 20's.

He'd gone hiking and hadn't returned the day he intended to. When we got the call, it was night, but we hiked in a few miles and set up camp on a ridge that had a pretty good view. He'd had gone into the woods prepared, so we decided to wait until daylight before beginning the search.

About 2 AM, I get up (for the bathroom) when I see a moving light a few miles away at the base of the cliffs across the valley. It looks like a flashlight, but we make the decision to keep waiting until daylight.

The following morning, we decide to go and check out the area and bring this guy home. We get to approximately where I saw the light the night before and start to call his name.

Quickly we find his body at the base of the cliff. His body was mangled. He'd fallen 60ft on his head. We radioed back that it had now become a recovery instead of rescue. At this point, the other ranger yells at me to come look. Lying 20ft from the man's body was his flashlight. It seemed odd, but I thought nothing of it. It kind of gave me the creeps, but I dismissed it.

When the coroner arrived, he said the man had been dead for at least 48 hours before we found the body. All of the sudden the alarm went off in my head; I knew this couldn't be possible. I asked the coroner to review his work. Same result again. I tried to find an explanation for the light I had seen; perhaps other hikers? But, one S&R had stayed at the only trailhead there all night. No one had come or gone.'

'To this day, I have no clue what I saw that night but it freaks me out now.'

In another account; 'This was when I was 22. So, I was spending the week alone in the campground in Banff National Park, (in the Rocky Mountains). I was the only person renting a Lot there; it was completely empty but for me. On the 3rd night, I hear something outside my tent, right by my head. It sounds like a hoof rhythmically falling, not stomping. I feel something's awareness on me, it feels 'intelligent.'

I light some candles (one was the Patron Saint of lost causes, St. Judas) Finally, I fall asleep.

The next night...I wake up to light rain, and its pitch black and quickly I remember what happened the night before and I can sense I'm not alone. Now there are two hoofs I can hear falling gently near my head.

I can feel myself being stared at through the tent canvas. Again, I light candles, but I don't fall asleep until dawn. That morning when I get up, I see that a log has been taken from the firewood pile and placed upright, about 5 feet in front of my tent entrance. The entire campground is surrounded by a 6-foot-tall electrified bear fence! - The entire place! I was the only one camping there!?'

A few years ago, Mark Sidwells wrote to the Fortean Times magazine to relate his story. "In 1986, I was studying engineering at Brooklands technical college in Weybridge, Surrey. One evening I was walking along the path from college to the train station. Normally the footpath would have been heaving with students eager to get home, but I was alone. About a third of the way along the path I decided to relieve myself against a tree. As I did so, I looked back to see if anyone was coming. It was twilight, but light enough to see. Someone was coming from over the brow of the hill, but too far away to worry about, so I carried on.

I looked back again and noticed the figure had gained some 30-odd yards. Thinking that it must be someone on a bike to have travelled that distance so quickly, I took another glance before finishing and the figure had again gained a lot of ground. I walked back to the path. I took another glance, thinking I should have heard a chain, or tyres, and I was confronted by what can only be described as "The Grim Reaper."

It was over 8 feet tall. The figure was wearing a black cloak, which hung over the body in a triangular shape, with a hood over the face. I then realized I that every time I had seen the figure it had been motionless as it was now...'

Jeff Stevens wrote in, with a surprisingly similar story; "In 1999, I was living in Roslindale, Massachusetts. My house bordered the Arnold Arboretum, a park with fields and forest. I spent a large amount of time in there, walking and biking.

Around dusk one evening I was walking down from on top of one of the hills. The landscape in front was mostly field with occasional trees. A paved path runs around one side of the hill. I was headed towards the path. I was singing softly to myself as I descended, when I became aware of someone else in the vicinity.

Looking up, I saw someone moving at great speed along the path, coming from the left. Embarrassed to be caught singing I glanced down, but something struck me as strange. This figure was moving way too fast to have been walking, so I assumed he was on a bike. The problem was, I realized, that there was no sound of tires, or gears shifting - nothing. And why was someone riding a bicycle while wearing a long black cloak?

He was big and skimmed along without any evidence of a bike. He starred fixedly ahead and since our paths were at a 90 degree angle, I never saw his face clearly, just the hood covering it. The cloak had one unusual feature: I found it difficult to focus on; my eyes wouldn't stay in focus when I looked at it, they went blurry.

I remember thinking; "I must be seeing things," and closing my eyes for a second or two. When I opened them, the figure was still there and passed right in front of me. Then, he simply vanished.

I walked around for a while, to see if he had dodged behind a tree, or veered suddenly off course, or what. But there was no sign. My first thought afterwards was that I had seen the grim reaper on a bike. The incident has baffled me ever since."

In another case; "One night, a huge shadow wearing what looked like a cloak was moving across the ground of the field. The shadow had no source. It was moving ridiculously fast. I went in the direction it was going. Eventually I saw this thing again, but this time it was floating, in mid-air. It just seemed like it wasn't part of this world. It floated around, seeming it was looking into the trees in the forest by the field, and then it suddenly jumped sideways, again so fast, and vanished into thin air."

Another person, writes, "This was in broad daylight in the woods. It was standing near a trail, beside a tree. I thought it was a Goth kid! It was dressed in black and had a hood. When I rounded the corner, and came up toward it, it was gone. What has made these things become visible to some of us?"

Lawyer and experienced mountaineer, George Duncan claimed he saw "the Devil himself there" on Ben Macdui, while descending from the mountain in the Scottish Highlands.

"All at once I got the shock of my life," Duncan stated, "before me (there was) a figure in a black robe – the conventional figure of the Devil himself!"

And yet, again, they are not always all-black. One lady described her experience close to the woods which lay just beyond her house. "I thought it to be a ghost. It was similar to the "Hat-man" descriptions in that it was certainly human-shaped. We had only recently moved there and had been there only a few weeks when we had come home late this night. There are no street lights out here so it's very dark.'

'We were letting the dogs out and the phone rang so my husband went back inside to answer it. One of the dogs went inside with him. I waited for the other dog outside. As we were walking back toward the front of the house, she suddenly stopped and began to bark like crazy. Her fur was all up and she was backing away. I looked up and I saw a white, human-looking figure peering around the corner of the house.'

'I could see the head very clearly, and dark circles or just voids where the eyes and the mouth would have been. I could also see what appeared to look like a hand, resting on the side of the house as it peered around at us. I could not see feet. I scooped the dog up and ran inside.'

'Years later, when my son was still young, he would talk about "the man in the woods who would float"?'

In November 1904, the *West Gippsland Gazette* reported on the return of 'The ghost of Tondu,' in Glamorganshire.

'It has reasserted itself in the most aggressive manner. A respectable resident of the district was proceeding at midnight along a lonely, narrow road adjoining the deserted buildings of the abandoned colliery, when he was attacked by the unnatural monster.'

'The gentleman is muscular, but the sight which suddenly met his gaze at the far end of a bridge made him turn hot and cold. An exceptionally tall, cadaverous figure was standing there. A silent, motionless sentinel. The head, as the frightened observer describes it, was "like a death's-head covered with wrinkled parchment. The eyes were hollow sockets."

'Suddenly the thing advanced towards the trembling man. It approached toward him with long arms outstretched. It clasped him in a vice and then began an uncanny tussle in the darkness. The resident felt himself held as though in the folds of a python. He tried to flee, but could not escape from the power of this supernatural assailant - then it was - gone.'

In another strange incident; 'When I was a kid, I was big into UFOs, conspiracies, all that..... I was reading and watching stuff I really shouldn't have been at that age. One night, my dad was driving me home from somewhere, and we were listening to the radio in the car. People had been seeing UFOs, everywhere. I had seen a few before, or I thought I had, but this was new. There were hundreds of people who had seen them.'

'Now, this was late, it was around 3 a.m. I can't remember why we were out that late, but we were. So, I was watching the skies like crazy, trying to spot something, but no dice. We reached home and as I was walking from the car to the house, the whole area lit up purple for maybe about thirty seconds. All we heard was this amazing boom, then it was gone. I could see everything perfectly in that purple light, it was as bright as the sun.'

'The next day, I went exploring to see if I could see anything. Maybe it crashed and exploded! So I was wandering around these roads in the middle of nowhere, looking for crashed spaceships! and I met this guy. He was just standing there in the middle of the road. He was completely bald, and with a massive smile. Like the Joker.'

'He started talking to me about the lights in the sky, and different aliens and conspiracy theories. He had this really weird smell. He stank of it. I've never smelled anything like it before or since. After a few minutes of talking to him, I jumped on my bike and sped home, totally freaked out.'

'It was a perfectly straight road for about half a mile. Every time I looked back, he was staring at me, watching me go.'

In a story that is very reminiscent of a long story in my previous book "Panic in the Woods," in which 2 college boys are chased through swamps and rivers by an entire group of people including women and children, who then kidnapped one of them and performed animal sacrifices and rubbed the blood all over him, before he managed to escape, another man describes some strange events that took place in the woods outside of the small rural town he grew up in.

'I grew up in this tiny crazy religious town. When I was about 9, me and a group of my friends decided to go into a small church to say a prayer. Yeah; well, I was only 9. Anyway, once inside we all took a look around and it got wacky. Two of us somehow got locked into the place behind the altar, someone else got locked in the toilet, and two got stuck in the baby-room.'

'A man heard us shouting for help and ran in, and he later said that someone in a mask ran out as soon as they saw him coming. He left behind two cans of petrol inside the church. Whoever it was got away.'

'Well, time passed, I grew up and moved away. A few months ago, I moved back. I only recently got my driving licence, and before that, a friend would take me out driving everyday as practice for the test. One day, he decided to head up a nearby mountain, to see how I could do up a really beat up track. I was driving around for a few hours, no problems, and then we saw a car crash in the distance.'

'The car was stuck in a dyke at the side of the road, with two people lying on the ground on either side. I naturally slow the car down to stop to see if we can help, and my friend takes out a knife and says: "If you stop this car, I will stab you. Keep moving..."

'So I did. I told him to take out his phone to call an ambulance but he kept looking behind him and then all around. It was weird, but I wasn't really thinking straight.'

'After moving maybe 50 feet away from the crash, I looked in the mirror. The two people on the ground; they're standing up and waving to the side. As I watch, about 8 people emerge from the forest, all in the same mask as the guy who trapped us in the church.'

'I shifted straight up through the gears and got out of there. A couple tried chasing after us, but no way was I stopping for anything. We went to the cops, and got laughed out of there.

We didn't hear of any disappearances or attacks, so we had nothing to back us up, until last week.'

'See, there's a lot of hippies and itinerants living on that mountain. I went to school with a few of them, they were okay, I got along alright with them. I met one last week in a bar. Hadn't seen him in years, we bought a few drinks and had a laugh. He told me that over the past few months, some new people started moving in on the mountain.'

'The hippies own the land free and clear, but as long as you didn't cause trouble, anyone can come and go as they please. They had a talk with a few of the new people, apparently they'd been in the area years back, but had some trouble with the law. Hippies didn't care, so long as they don't cause trouble they can stay there. Then a little girl, about 10, came running into their camp, cut and bruised, clothes torn; she was completely terrified.'

He now thinks they staged the car crash to try to lure potential victims in.....

In another account; 'When I was in 8th grade, two teachers and my class went on a one night camp trip where we would do activities like kayaking and trail hiking. I'm in New South Wales and live about an hour from a national forest that was notorious for 'the backpacker murders.' Several bodies have been found and many more are still missing. It's pretty certain all of the murders were by the same serial killer.'

'Anyway, that morning we left for the forest in a school bus and when we reached the road that leads to the forest entrance, there's a police car parked there. He talked to the teachers for a couple of minutes but we couldn't hear what he said. No-one said anything about it and we were all talking anyway'.

'Fast forward to about two hours later and we've set up the camp and been for a short trek. That afternoon we notice a helicopter circling while we're kayaking, but again we don't think anything specially about it. Me and a couple of friends get out of the water and start making rafts by the water's edge and we see a park ranger come and pull one of the instructors to the side and they're talking in hushed tones. He looks a bit stressed. I know i heard the instructor say, "You're kidding!" and he looked kinda shocked.'

'At this point I'm starting to connect the dots but I don't say anything to my friends. At dusk, I'd needed to go use the toilet, which is about 120 meters from the campsite and I make my way over there. As I go in the toilet block I remember a guy walking around the other side but I didn't see him clearly. He was acting a bit nervous, glancing around. I didn't recognise him and so he wasn't with us. To me he didn't fit, but I didn't think too much of it at the time.'

'Fast forward to the next morning and we're heading back to the car park to leave. When we get there, our teacher tells us that a body was found in the river, not far from where we were. He said they didn't want to tell us so as not to frighten us. We later found out it was a young guy, and the guy who killed him was related to the serial killer who had hunted the same area.

I can't say if the man i saw at the toilets had anything to do with it; but i haven't been camping since.'

In another account; 'I was in 5th grade. There's a sewer drain/entrance covered in satanic/devil graffiti and a circle about fifty yards in the tunnel/sewer just beyond the edge of our neighbourhood, in the wooded area. I tell friends at school how cool I am that older kids have showed me this place, but they won't believe it unless I show them myself, so after school we ride our bikes over there.'

'We drop our bikes at the top of the hill and start walking down to the creek/bayou where the storm drain dumped out. My friends are laughing and talking with each other behind me. I start to hear whispers up ahead of me; at first my friends think I'm wimping out, but then they hear the whispers as well.'

'All of us stopped, straining our ears to hear when three dudes, early-thirties, jump up out of the bushes and sprint full speed at us. We turn around, run, grab our bikes and book it. We look back to see the guys right on our heels.'

'Slowly we're building distance between us but the guys are still giving chase, and they followed us about two miles back to the neighbourhood. I don't know if they were connected to the tunnel or just three crack heads we interrupted, but I never went back there.'

'A couple of months later, I'm at the neighbourhood pool for a swim meet, and it's getting dark. One of the kids says he is bored and going to walk home. Later, his mom comes over to see where he is, and we reply that he went home to play games. She's indifferent, until we mention he walked through woods to go home and she becomes terrified.'

'She gets her husband and other fathers to do an immediate search of the woods, well it turns out the kid was home safe, but we never found out what the adults knew about that area and the woods....'

Epping Forest in Essex, England, is one of the most ancient woodlands and was once a hide-out for the fearsome female warrior Boudicea. In fact, this fearsome warrior, facing defeat with the imminent arrival of a more fortified enemy, drank poison in the forest to kill herself rather than concede defeat to her foe.

There's a long road on a hill in the forest. It's called 'Hangman's Hill,' and it's here that apparitions have been reported of a man being seen in the woods. He has a sinister smile on his face and he is holding up a noose. In the 17th and 18th centuries, the forest was the location for the hanging of hundreds of men, hung for their crimes.

The famous Highwayman Dick Turpin once hid out in the woods, and also used it as a lair from which to rob passing carriages of travellers. The forest, ever since this time, has a long-held standing for its criminal associations.

The forest's proximity to London has made it notorious as a burial site for murder victims. Triple-police killer, Harry Roberts hid out in the forest. In the sixties, 15-year-old school girl Marian Hartley was dragged into the forest by an abductor as she was returning home from a dance, and her killer left her body there. In the 1980's, accountant Terence Gooderham and his girlfriend Maxine Arnold, were taken into the forest and shot hit-man-style with a double-barrelled shotgun. In the 90's, massage parlour owner Patricia Parsons, was found dead in her car having been shot in the head with a cross-bow. In 2000, 31-

year-old Wendy Woodhouse, was taken to the forest, tortured and beaten to death with a snooker cue by two men.

 In 2015, a murder inquiry was launched after a body was found "wrapped in an Ikea bag" near lake in Epping Forest. According to newspaper reports, a person out walking in the forest made the "grim discovery after coming across a horrific smell and a pack of rats." Police confirmed the remains had been found partially buried in the woods. The walker was reported to have seen dozens of rats scurrying around the trees and when he approached to investigate he saw the decomposing body.

Over the years, a number of people have died near 'Hangman's Hill.' Sometimes they aren't discovered until a few days later. Every now and then drivers say they saw a person walking in the middle of the road and have had to slam on their brakes to prevent hitting the figure. Cars roll up hill there on their own for an unknown reason.

East London Guardian Newspaper reported on the case of 11-year-old Jack Brody, who in May 2012 noticed something very strange in the sky over the forest. Quickly he ran inside his home and grabbed a camera and began to take photographs of a silver object. When he later showed his father, his father was unimpressed at first, despite the excitement of his son. "I came back from a walk and he ran up to me saying; "You will not believe what I got a picture of!"

'He pointed at this thing that was so small that you could barely see it. It was up there glimmering in the sun. But – when we zoomed in and looked more closely I said to my friend who was with me, "You have to see this!" - We just could not work out what it was. It was this silver circular thing. Some people may say that it must have been a weather balloon, but the way it moved, I just don't think it could have been."

"When a plane came close to it, it was there one minute and the next minute it was gone - you could not hear it fly off, you just could not see it again."

"Committed UFO spotters who spend years trying to get pictures would not be able to get one that is that good! It was extremely odd."

Terrifying screams have been heard around the outskirts of the forest, which sometimes suggests that there is more going on than gangland style murders. People who have gone to the forest have also reported feeling as though they are being choked. There's also one more very mysterious feature in the ancient forest, though its precise location is elusive. It's the 'Suicide Pool.'

Two centuries ago, an Irish writer described finding a haunted pool in Epping Forest, but he refused to reveal its location. He said it was too evil and far too dangerous. According to Terry Carter of the Loughton & District Historical Society Newsletter, the Essex Countryside (Magazine) in 1959, was requesting readers to write in with any information about the location of this Suicide Pool. Several people responded, claiming that they knew exactly where it was, but not one of them were willing to disclose which of the ponds inside the forest was the curséd one.

Carter, of the historical society says; "One good lady refused point-blank to divulge the exact location, insisting that it was too wicked and dangerous a place to reveal the truth. She wrote; "The pool is deep in the forest and birds are never heard here, squirrels and deer shun it. It is a dark and evil and malignant place. The atmosphere there is unpleasant beyond description. The waters are black...."

Carter says that those who found themselves unwittingly at the pond, with no knowledge of its sinister reputation, but no matter how rational, would always leave, running from the pond. Others were less fortunate, as it's said that some who found themselves there felt an overpowering urge to commit suicide by drowning themselves. It has been the scene of mysterious tragedies. People known to have no inclination to commit suicide, have been discovered dead there.

He adds, "Scepticism is perhaps in order; however, I do remember my grandfather, who knew the woods there like the back of his hand, warning me and my friends at various times to be careful of wandering anywhere near a certain location, because he told us "there were horrible things that sometimes happened."

Chapter 10: Half-man Half-beast

Roger Marsh has been covering MUFON's incoming cases since January 2009. Case number 83325 involves the curious witness report from a woman who was out on Lake Michigan with her husband and a group of friends, on the night of April 16th, 2017. They were celebrating one of their birthday's and they were having a great time when one of them spotted something in the sky above them.

"We were about 2 miles out on the lake and I looked up and saw what looked like a giant bat. It was as tall as my husband, whose 6ft 4! It was blacker than the night sky. It was solid black, with eyes that seemed to reflect the moonlight. It circled our boat three times in total silence before heading away. It blended into the night and then was gone in seconds."

The witness also adds that five minutes later, "a bright green object was moving across the horizon. It wasn't a plane - it was bright green! And it was moving slowly. After it disappeared out of sight, we just sat there in silence, stunned."

"I began to feel this overwhelming sensation of dread. I told my husband that I felt we should get off the water as quickly as possible."

Thirty minutes later, another report came in. This witness, whose case number is 83243 in MUFON records, said he was hanging out in Chicago with friends. They were all chatting outside, when suddenly; "We heard what sounded like a bird flapping its wings. One of my homies yelled like he saw a huge Lechuza!" A Lechuza is a witch, or 'bruja,' in Mexican folklore, who can turn into a giant black bird.

 "We walked over and saw what looked like an owl but it stood up and it was about 6ft tall! It looked right at us. It had large glowing red eyes that were completely freaking us all out."

Six days prior to this, on the 10th of April, someone else had a very unsettling encounter, also in Chicago. She contacted the 'UFO clearing house' organisation, to relate what had happened to her, although reluctant to do so, but she could make no sense of what had happened to her. She wondered if anyone could help her come to terms with what she'd faced, and explain or identify it. This report was picked up by Tobias Wayland, another member of MUFON and who runs the blog *The Singular Fortean*.

"On the street to the park (Oz Park) my dog began acting very peculiarly. She was practically being dragged as she resisted. I noticed that many of the birds you usually hear were silent. I heard the flapping of wings. I assumed it would be Canadian Geese. Then something caught my eye and what I saw scares the …. out of me still."

"I saw a large man standing there, 7 ft or taller. He was solid black, and a large pair of wings were folded behind him. These wings stood taller than the man, by at least a foot. They jutted out of his back."

"I could not see his face as it was turned away from me and perhaps didn't notice me. Then it turned and I saw bright, ruby red eyes that appeared to glow from within. It faced me. It was 7 feet tall and instead of clothes, it looked like a giant half-man half-bird. It stared at me for what felt like eternity. I felt like it could see right through me. That it could read me, that it knew what I was thinking, like it could see into my soul. It was terrifying."

"It unfurled its wings and screeched, really loud and jetted into the air. The wings were at least 10 feet from tip to tip. I do not take drugs. I know what I saw was real. I want to warn others. I never felt I was in danger – if I did not provoke it, but, I felt it could rip me apart…"

A person who read the account replied, "There are many stories of this unidentified birdman. I've also read accounts where someone climbed a mountain and found a cave they saw a big bird-like man fly to and found human bones. All I can say is I wish mainstream media would warn people to hold onto small children and pets! Many insiders on Aliens say that some of the species want to eat us and that humans wouldn't be able to handle this knowledge."

Chapter 11: More go missing

Humboldt University Student, 20-year-old Michael Madden, had plans to become a forest ranger.

On August 10th, 1996, he had made plans to meet his friends at San Bar Flat, on the Stanislaus River near Sonora, in the Stanislaus National Forest, California, to go fishing and camping. It was a spot at which he and his father had camped many times before when growing up, and he was therefore very familiar with the area.

When his friends arrived at the spot, at approximately 2 a.m. on the 12th August, they were surprised to find no sign of Michael there. However, his camping and fishing gear was there, along with a freshly made fire. Not long after that, a man appeared. He was carrying a .45 automatic and he asked the group of friends, "Are you looking for Mikey?"

He continued to stand there, and began to cock his gun, repeatedly. He stayed with them for hours that night. He appeared to be wearing boots that looked very much like the ones Michael wore.

It was after this that his friends officially reported him missing. The police arrived and scoured the area extensively with search and rescue including dogs and divers. Any clues about the missing young man's whereabouts however, were not found. Four days later, his dog returned to the spot, dehydrated, but was unable to lead searchers to where Michael might be.

The man who had repeatedly cocked his pistol was identified as Joseph Tine, and he was given a polygraph test. The results were never revealed, but police never arrested him. His gun had no spent shells. This encounter, certainly for the missing man's friends however, sounds like a scene from a horror movie. It had to have been extremely creepy and very unsettling.

Had this man done something to Michael? How did he know Michael's name? Why did he call him "Mikey?" – a name none of his friends called him. Was he attempting to make it sound that they had become acquainted and become friends, before his own friends had got there? Or, was it intended to creep them out, calling him "Mikey," as though taunting them, fully in the knowledge that he had done something sinister to their friend and finding it entertaining to watch them squirm?

According to reports from the Bee newspaper at the time of the young man's disappearance, some witnesses said they had seen him sitting along the banks of the river, the day that he got there, with his dog. His friends then arrived the next day. That was believed to have been the last sighting of him. "There was a camp-fire lit," one of his friends, Josh Rocha told the police and newspaper reporters, at the time.

"Some creepy guy popped out of the bushes and he said; "What are you doing here?" Then he asked them if they were looking for "Mikey." The thing was, none of them ever called him Mikey.

Michael's step-brother, Randy Powell said that police reports at the time included statements from witnesses who told the authorities that Michael had been seen at a cabin near an area called Pinecrest, rather than Sand Bar, on the day he disappeared. As for the police, they formed the opinion that with no sign of Michael, despite their extensive searches of the area, he was most likely murdered.

Over the years, with still no body showing up and no further evidence at all to go on, they wondered, had he fallen victim to a random killer, who happened to be in the area? or even a serial killer such as the then unknown Cary Stayner, who was later convicted of killing several hikers in the Yosemite national Park, approximately one hour away, in the 1990's.

In fact, his father, who would call the local reporters over the passing years, often in tears because he could not understand why there were no breaks in his son's case and calling the police when searches were being carried out for the missing tourists in the national park. His father died without ever finding out what happened to his son.

Could he have fallen into the river? And yet, divers had been brought in, and thorough searches conducted, and no body found. In May 2016, a person out walking saw what turned out to be human remains. Investigators from the County Sheriff's office later confirmed that they were human remains but they could have belonged to any number of people who had vanished at the same spot.

The Modesto Bee listed a number of people who had mysteriously disappeared there, as well as Michael. In August 2005, Mrs Nita Mayo, a 67-year-old lady from Hawthorne, Nevada, also disappeared in the same area. Her car was found at Donnell Vista Point. Her purse and cell-phone were inside, along with a receipt from a general store, 10 miles away, but when dogs searched the vista point area, they picked up no scent of her other than right at the car.

Search teams found no trace of her, and no clues that could indicate where she could have possibly gone. Strangely, almost like in Madden's case, an unidentified man went to the Medical Clinic where she worked after she disappeared, on the day her car was found. He showed up at the clinic and claimed that he had heard Mrs Mayo had vanished but that she had been found. She had not been found, and in fact, the search for her had not even begun at that point.

The missing woman's daughter Tracy says, "He was really weird." She also added that he was interviewed and failed a polygraph, but added that he was not arrested. Then the case went cold as winter set in.

She could not let it rest however. She held on to the possibility that this person knew more than the police had told her, and several years after her mother disappeared, she drove to his home town and showed up at his workplace, in Texas.

She told the *Modesto Bee*; "I went alone, which probably wasn't too smart and I didn't tell him I was coming." Creepily she says, "When he saw me, I didn't say a word. He said, "Hello, Tracy. How are you?""

She spoke with him but she says that when she left, she knew no more than when she had set out to question him. He offered nothing that would implicate himself in any way and she found nothing he said to be incriminating.

In April 2014, 46 -year-old Patty Sue Tolhurst vanished. Her car was found at the same spot at the Vista point. By this time, she'd been reported missing for a week. Police believed she had been en-route to meet a friend. The Sheriff's Office later said that on April 20th, the day she disappeared, she'd sent a letter to some friends stating that she was going to be doing some hiking up in the area that her car was found.

CBS local for Sacramento covered the story of the missing woman. 'A mother of two and owner of popular café vanished without a trace!' They said that at the time, everyone believed 'She had left to get groceries after her cafe ran out and that she would be straight back,' but 'She never came back.' (although we know that the police later revealed she had mailed a letter to friends saying she was going hiking, according to the Sheriff's office.)

'Her SUV would later be found abandoned at the remote vista point, 30 miles east of Sonora. Her purse was still inside. It was abandoned, and the sunroof left open. It had been rained in.'

Search and Rescue teams found no clues near her car. She had however, as well as the letter, sent "two rambling audiotapes to friends."

When her father was interviewed, he said that he hoped it was just a case that she needed some time away for herself. However, with each day that passed, his concern continued to grow....

In October 2016, another person vanished from Donell Vista point in the Stanislaus National Forest. Sixty-eight year old Breck Phelps disappeared there while on a fishing trip.

His car was found a quarter of a mile away near a trail leading down to the River. Several search and rescue teams joined the search mission for him, including additional personnel across the entire state. The search effort comprised dog teams, and a National Guard helicopter, with infrared thermal imaging.

Phelps was discovered to be missing after a friend became worried about him not returning, and drove out to the vista point. It was an area that the 68-year-old liked to go to, to hike and to fish. His friend found his car parked there but no sign of his friend at the scene nor near the river. A boat was called in to search the river and reservoir.

Not long after unidentified human remains had been found, in 2016, the Tuolumne County Sheriff's office ruled out any connection between them and any of the missing people.

District Ranger Molly Fuller has said of the mystery of the place; "It's a day-use area, not a campground, so you can't stay here overnight. It is dangerous, but there's a lot of dangerous places in the forest," Fuller said. "There's really no explanation for why people have parked there and disappeared. I have no explanation."

As the *Union Democrat journal* writes; 'The vista point, in Stanislaus National Forest, is mystifying. Many have travelled there to marvel at the magnificence of the landscape... a few have never returned.'

Let's end now on perhaps what is the most mysterious story I have ever heard; Joan Grant was a historical novelist who also wrote of the most vivid recollections of past lives she believed she'd had. She was also prone to experiencing things of a more paranormal nature, that she couldn't account for. One such incident occurred in the 1920's when she went to the Cairngorms National Park in Scotland. According to her autobiography *Time out of Mind*, she was staying with her husband Leslie at a shooting lodge, near Grantown-on-Spey in Scotland, in August 1928.

They set out from Rothiemurchus, in the heart of the National Park, intending to climb toward the Mountains, but it was such a beautifully hot day that she and her husband opted to laze in the sun and eat a picnic in the forest there. Then they took a leisurely stroll before leaving to go back to the hotel. "It was too peaceful for serious walking. Nothing could have been further from my mind than spooks when suddenly I was seized with such terror that in panic I turned and fled back along the path."

Her husband, completely non-plussed by her flight, ran after her, shouting at her, trying to find out what was wrong. She could only just find enough breath to tell him; "Run!"

"Something malign, four-legged yet obscenely human, invisible but solid enough for me to hear pounding hooves trying to reach me. If it did I would die. I ran on for about half a mile when I burst through some invisible barrier and I knew then I was safe while seconds before I had been in mortal danger."

"A year later one of my father's professors described an almost exact experience he'd had; he was a rationalist but he had been so profoundly startled by the experience that he had written to the Newspaper *The Times*; and, received a letter from another reader, who had also been pursued by this "Thing."

"Years later, the Professor told me about two hikers for whom search parties had been out for three days, then they had been found dead. He showed me the exact spot on the map at which they had been found. It was the same place as my terror. Both of the men had been under the age of thirty. The weather had been fine. They had spent a night under shelter of a stone-shelter and written in the visitor book there. They were found within 100 yards of each other, sprawled face down as though they had fallen headlong when in flight."

"I did a post-mortem on them both," the Professor, a Doctor, told me gravely. "Never in my life had I seen healthier corpses; there was not a thing wrong with either of the chaps except their hearts stopped. I put 'heart failure' on the chit, but it is my considered opinion that they died of fright…."

Excerpts from other books by Steph Young-

Excerpts from Stalked in the Woods;

In Volume 3. of the 1947 Round Robin Bulletin of Contact and Information from the Borderland Sciences Research Foundation, comes a strange story sent into them and presented at a Conference for scrutiny. The editors of the bulletin found the man's account to appear to be of veracity, including the photographs he provided to supplement his account. They also add as a word of caution, that any ideas of investigating the area he talks about as "bold adventurers armed with machine guns" might well be "disastrous folly."

Mr E. Johns had contacted them to tell of his experiences, which occured when he moved to the area of the Mendocino Mountain Range in California in 1930 with his mother, to make a homestead there. Once they had purchased the land, they built a very basic home and decided to have some of the forest cut down close to the house in order to sell firewood to raise the funds they needed to finish their home to a higher standard.

They hired a lumberjack to chop down some of the trees, and Johns and his mother made the journey to the closest town to sell the firewood. They were away for two days. When they returned, the lumberjack came up to them, told them to keep the bond money he had given them as a 'promise' that he would complete their work for them, and said he would not continue the work nor would he ever come back there. He would not explain to them his reason; he simply told them that under no circumstance would he ever return there.

All was well for the first few nights after he left. Then things began to get very strange. "We could hear noises that did not belong; many horses drinking water though there was no water; I didn't have a water supply, and when I went outside I saw nothing. The door knob would turn of its own accord. I shot through the door and then it quit. There was a phenomenon of bright lights at night over the house, as though there was a streetlamp and as though the place had moved to town. It stayed like that all night but I was never able to find out where they came from.

A couple of weeks later, I was introduced to the little people. At first I thought they were figments of my imagination. I would soon learn better. They were followed by what I now know are Undines and Sylphs. They would surround me. They would ask me childish questions such as "What is a gun?" I asked them where they live and they showed my all of the secrets they were allowed to. It appeared that the land I had was in the centre of their domain and that it changes into their vibration at times; but that if I were to enter their land I would be unable to return.

The secrets are not for the average person to know and so I would rather not tell them. I have been given the power to find all secrets. There is no secret that I cannot find if I wish to and technical things that are far beyond anything science has today; but many of these things should be forgotten I feel, for the people are not ready for such knowledge yet. I have lived with these things now and have been very lucky to escape alive. My luck may not protect everyone who goes into such a world. I tried to get a tree Nymph to come with me, but the 'ruling power' would not allow this to happen. I see now why, but I did not at the time.

In the kitchen window at sundown one day, we saw a pair of eyes staring at us. They were five inches in diameter. They glowed reddish, very bright. When I went outside I saw nothing; they had vanished. When I went back in the house, they reappeared. This game continued for twenty minutes. Then they went away. While they were going away we saw a large shape like three large cones piled one on top the other. This shape went across the meadow. I never found out what that was.

One night, at around 10 p.m. we saw two cars drive down the road to the end, or so we thought. The road they were on was a narrow trail that ends at a Canyon, with no way to turn around. You have to back up all the way. The next morning we followed the car tracks. They ended against a boulder and that was that. Never did learn where they went. I have had hints since then, but I do not care to enlarge upon them. Several "perfect crimes" have been committed here. A man murdered two wives near the Canyon. He was later found dead in his car with the doors shut and windows locked. One empty rifle was in his hands and a loaded rifle beside him. The coroner never did find out what killed him.

Also there is a phenomenon. When you try to walk up the mountain it's like walking through molasses, and when you go down you are pushed down faster than you would wish. Some are bodily thrown as far as twenty feet." After he moved away from the area, he returned on many occasions. "There is an undercurrent of fear in the area that is intangible but noticed in the people who live in the fringes of the area. Ranches have been abandoned. It is useless to fight the spirits. Anyone who attempts to build a home here it seems, usually comes to grief, one way or another, and we have been no exception to the rule; however, we were smart enough to get out while still able."

Say the Editors of the Journal to which the man sent in the story of his experiences which occurred; "The phenomena of the lights and the huge eyes have many parallels. We have no reason to question the correctness of his accounts as far as our information stands. Phenomena of this type do not call for an

135

expedition with guns; for any folly of that sort might well be disastrous…."

Excerpt from Panic in the Woods

Chapter 3: "Whatever it was, it hitched a ride back to where I live."

Recently I was contacted by a man called Chris Nash. He had a very strange and rather disturbing set of photographs. They had been taken in Rendlesham forest, and at his home, because whatever had been in the forest had followed him home. The photos appear to display a demon. Or, an alien. Whatever it is, the malevolence is clear to see in its yellow eyes amid the darkness of the forest at night. It appears to have an angular face, deep set bright eyes. It is not fully clear but the eyes are there to see. "Whatever it was, it hitched a ride back to where I live, as I've had a presence at my house ever since. Not a nice presence…"

"In the forest I've experienced voices, shadow people, strange lights, the feeling of being sick like death. Personally I had a night where I was walking up a well-known path back to my car and I heard something whisper my name, then I felt a presence. A few seconds later, it was bearing down on my back. After this I had a feeling of being terrified. I was told by a medium I was playing with fire if I kept going back to the forest and something bad would happen if I continued to go. Not that that put me off."

Now however, he feels he may regret his continued visits to the forest at night. "I've got something here at the house that wants a piece of me…. A friend is saying its possibly a succubus, a demon. I heard a growl the other day in my front room, and this morning in bed I couldn't breathe, and it felt like something was pressing down on my chest. I feel like I've got a battle going on in my mind. Is this the battle we all face? Good vs Evil? I'm sleeping with the lights on and it seems OK…..Strange; maybe the light puts them off? I know they love the dark. Demons look like what's in the photograph. Can you see the horns? It looks like a devil; you tell me?"

It did indeed look like a demon. In fact, I've never seen anything quite like or, or as disturbing. It's a very disturbing photograph. A sense of evil pervades the image and it's impossible to deny that it looks anything other than a demon, or alien, but a gut, instinctive feeling leans toward the demonic. It feels very uncomfortable to look at it, as though it is acknowledging it and welcoming its presence just by doing so; as if it is a taboo and cursed thing to do. Perhaps that is just superstition, but then, I wouldn't want to test that theory.

He showed me another photograph; "When I woke up one morning, there was this mark: - there's 6 fingers." The photograph shows six marks on his skin. They look like red finger marks, left on the skin from pressing hard down on it. There are six finger marks, not five....

Chris has been visiting Rendlesham Forest for several years now, sometimes several times a week. It's a couple of hours drive from where he lives to get there, but something keeps drawing him back, despite the warnings and the dark sinister attachment he now seems to have in his house. He took the photographs to a local medium. She insisted he take the photographs out of her house immediately. She told him she would not have them in her house; so strongly did she feel that it was an entity captured in the photos, of a power she did not want to be confronted with.

Though Chris wants help, he feels torn between whether asking for help would make his current situation worse. He says he is torn between exorcism or spiritual cleansing. He fears goading the entity. He also feels he can manage with the situation, but only time will tell if that is the case. Of the entities he says he has seen in the forest at night, he asks, could they all be malevolent or could any of them be good? Like with people, perhaps both benevolent and malevolent spirits or entities occupy the forest. Nature spirits who mean no ill-will perhaps, spirits of the departed returning maybe, but alongside these there may be mischievous and ill-intending darker forces.

It's by the East Gate of the forest that Chris and his friends have experienced most activity. It was there that he captured the demonic face in the photograph. He said he could feel a presence before he reached for his camera. That presence has now followed him home, and often now, he feels something is standing behind him. In the forest he says he has seen dark shadow people fleeting out of the corner of his eyes; it was one of the first things he noticed in the forest when strange things began happening. He's seen, and captured on film, orbs, and also white streaks that resemble ectoplasm or phantasms. Though he has not seen anything that resembles Extra Terrestrials; several of those in his group have, and on many occasions.

He and his friends began to go there at night, initially drawn to the place after the famous Rendlesham Forest incident. They wanted to explore it at night. Often they would go there, light a bonfire and camp out. They visited other forests too; but this was the one that seemed teeming with activity that does not come from our world. Of all of his experiences there, it is the demonic entity that has most disturbed him. Perhaps even more alarming, Chris says he wonders if the Demon is tempting him. There have been instances where he has had reason to think badly of other people; circumstances in his life, like in everyone's life, where harmonious relationships sometimes turn bad due to the actions of others, and our thoughts toward them become angry. We may even wish them harm: mentally, and even physically.

It's our natural instinct to seek vengeance as our thoughts turn to revenge against those who may have hurt us. In Chris's case, he did harbour bad thoughts towards someone; only this time, he wonders if his negative thoughts turned into reality. He wonders; did his darkest wishes manifest into action? - Someone died, and he'd been wishing them dead. Then it happened another time. He fears there is a spiritual battle between good and evil going on inside his head. He feels he is being offered some form of supernatural power by the entity, and being tempted to take it. He feels the demon may be doing things for him, to prove how much power he could have if he made a deal with it and allowed him in. He even accepts how good it would be to accept that deal, to have that power.....but he won't do that deal.

One of the people Chris goes to the forest with is a lady called Brenda Butler. She's been going there for many years. Chris says she has captured even more images than him; a multitude of strange images in photographs taken inside the forest. Orbs, strands of misty white, faces, dark shapes, and many other unidentifiable anomalies. Brenda Butler has been going to the Forest for decades. She gave a lecture in 2010, in which she described an incident in November, 1979; a year prior to the famous Rendlesham Forest incident, in which U.S. Air-force security witnessed what they believe, was a U.F.O. landing in the forest.

In 1979, Ms Butler was living on a farm at Aldringham (20 minutes from the Forest). "That night a craft came down in the field. It was 3 a.m. My father also saw it. The next morning there were broken tree-tops, and holes and marks in the fields. At the end of November, local people were saying they'd seen UFO's. People came forward to say they'd seen little monks, little people..... A Rabbit Catcher said he saw some little figures. He immediately phoned the RAF base security – he thought they were little children in fancy dress. The RAF security guards came out and went toward them – the figures vanished. The Rabbit Catcher said he was then arrested and taken to the base and questioned. After that, he was reluctant to report it when he had other sightings."

In January, 1980, the UFO reports continued, she said. When she heard of the Rendlesham Forest Incident experienced by the American security guards, she says there were several independent English witnesses to it too. At 11 a.m. on the day after the sighting, a man told her he was out walking his dog when he came across three men in what he said were 'silver' firemen's outfit - or at least, he assumed they were firemen, although he knew British fireman do not wear silver. He said it was bright lights that had drawn him to them, and as he approached the lights through the woods, he hid behind a tree, and from there he could see the three figures.

He said he saw a silver 'missile-type thing' on the forest floor, and the three men were covering it over with some kind of tarpaulin. He had refused to talk after this initial report however, said Ms Butler; he was scared, and he said he'd been warned not to talk. He added that he didn't think it was a UFO. "We've seen greys here," she says. "We've seen them walking. They've stood beside us. We've seen them working – I don't know what they were doing. I think they were building something. They were taking things away. I think they go to another dimension. Myself and an American have had missing time here - I don't know what happened, but we lost four hours. We were walking down a trail. We saw a big white light. It split apart into 3 lights, then they re-merged into one light." "A helicopter came over the trees, chasing it. We were watching it chasing it toward the sea. When we went to leave the forest, nothing looked the same. There were no trees, no familiar sights. We walked for ages and ages. We couldn't find our way back – the area wasn't the same. It was just like open fields. No trees, no bushes. We didn't know where we were or what was happening. Eventually, we did get back to the car.

We drove round to where we believed we had been – and everything was normal; the trees, the bushes, everything. I've been with a friend in the Forest, walking together along-side each other and the next minute I'm right across on the other side of the forest; - in seconds I've gone right across the Forest."

"Other people have told me they've been dragged down into an underground tunnel by E.T.'s – I don't believe that. We've looked everywhere but we can't find any tunnels. There are portals – we have photos of that. I have photos of E.T.'s coming out of the portals."

Given her 30 years of experiences within the Forest, she has written a book based on her investigations, called 'Sky Crash through Time; a continued investigation into the Rendlesham UFO mystery.'

On Sunday, January 25th, 2015, a dog walker believes he captured a UFO in the sky above Rendlesham Forest. He posted the footage on the internet and the BBC contacted him to interview him. Local man George Taylor was walking in the Forest with his dog when he says, "I spotted three balls of light in the sky. Couldn't believe what I was seeing. I had a weird feeling that I shouldn't be there. I recorded it on my phone and uploaded it to see if anyone else witnessed anything similar yesterday. Very strange! Anyone have any idea what it may be? I know the Forest has a long history of this but I didn't really believe in it as I haven't seen anything odd in all the years I've lived here - until this. I regularly take my dogs for a walk here and I've never seen anything as strange as this."

The footage shows three dancing Orbs in the sky above him, above the clouds but in clear daylight. Strangely, there is a low flying helicopter going over the forest at the same time. People have suggested it's a stunt, or a fake, or it's flares; but flares can't behave that way....

Excerpt from Something in the Woods is Taking People:

In the U.K. in 1980. Zygmunt Adamski disappeared from Todmorden in the rural county of Yorkshire on June 6, 1980 after leaving his house.

Five days later his body was located on the top of a coal pile in a coal mine.

The police attended the scene, where on examination they found burn marks on the man's shoulders and neck, and a strange green ointment covering the wounds. The ointment was never able to be scientifically identified.

His clothes were clean despite him having been missing for five days, although his jacket had been buttoned up incorrectly and his shirt was missing. There were no footprints in the coal.

The Mine Company's son was the last person in the area, but he'd been there before midday. He had seen no body on a coal pile. It appeared to have been put there after that time.

The pathologist ruled that his death had occurred between eleven and one pm of that day, but the burns on his body were determined to have occurred two days before his death.

He stated, "What led to his death couldn't be answered," but he ruled that the man had died of a heart attack due to shock or fright. His face had been contorted with fear.

The case was never solved any further than that, but oddly enough a few months after finding the man's body there, one of the policemen, Alan Godfrey, was on a night shift and claimed to have experienced an unnerving incident himself.

Searching for some missing cows, he claimed that he saw a strange large object in front of him in the road, hovering above the ground.

He tried to radio colleagues, but his radio went dead. Frightened, he remained in the car.

He was later to realise that over half an hour had passed that he couldn't account for, and he found that the soles of his boots were split wide open, looking to him as though he'd been dragged along the ground.

That same night other policemen independently called into headquarters with alarming reports of seeing bright lights descending into the valley, and a driver also called the police.

The cows were later discovered in a field which had been previously empty and the entrance gate to it was locked. The ground was muddy, but there were no prints from the cows. Like the man, it was as though they too had literally been dropped there.

The policeman himself was so disturbed by his experience that he underwent hypno-regression, in search of answers about what could have happened to him in the missing half an hour.

Under a state of hypnosis he began to describe being in a room with a black-robed, bearded man with a biblical appearance, accompanied by a huge black dog and other, Smaller 'Creatures' that were the size of five year olds and had robotic movements.

These intriguing cases are just the beginning...... there are many others in the collection of books I've written....
Added to this, I have now started a Podcast, appropriately called "Masquerade: Creepy Mysteries of the Unexplained." If you would like to, you can listen to Episodes on iTunes, or here;

New Exclusive Episodes will also be available only here; Patreon Steph Young Masquerade podcast

I have website; Stephyoungauthor.com if you would like to subscribe to my mailing list, to stay up to date with new releases.

I hope you have enjoyed this book and the strange collection of mysterious events. If you have enjoyed it, perhaps you would be kind enough to leave me a review,

Thank you, Steph

68011734R00093

Made in the USA
Columbia, SC
02 August 2019